ABIGAIL POPE

J. T. ROGERS

The Overwhelming

J. T. ROGERS is the author of *Madagascar*, *White People*, and other plays. His works have been produced in London by the National Theatre and Out of Joint, and on the radio for the BBC; in New York at the Roundabout Theatre and the Summer Play Festival; and regionally at the Philadelphia Theatre Company, the Road Theatre (Los Angeles), New Theatre (Coral Gables), the Adirondack Theatre Festival (New York), and many times at the Salt Lake Acting Company, where he was an NEA/TCG playwright in residence. His plays have recently won the Pinter Review Prize for Drama, the American Theatre Critics Association's M. Elizabeth Osborn Award, the William Inge Center for the Arts Otis Guernsey New Voices Award, and the Blanche and Irving Laurie Foundation's Theatre Visions Award. He lives in Brooklyn, New York.

—NOTES—

—NOTES—

The Overwhelming

The Overwhelming

A PLAY

J. T. Rogers

FABER AND FABER, INC.
AN AFFILIATE OF FARRAR, STRAUS AND GIROUX
NEW YORK

FABER AND FABER, INC.
An affiliate of Farrar, Straus and Giroux
19 Union Square West, New York 10003

Distributed in Canada by Douglas & McIntyre Ltd.
Printed in the United States of America
Originally published in 2006 in slightly different form by
Faber and Faber Limited, Great Britain
Published in the United States by Faber and Faber, Inc.
First American edition, 2007

Library of Congress Cataloging-in-Publication Data
Rogers, J. T., 1968–
The overwhelming / by J. T. Rogers. — 1st ed.
p. cm.
ISBN-13: 978-0-86547-974-6 (pbk. : alk. paper)
ISBN-10: 0-86547-974-7 (pbk. : alk. paper)
1. Americans—Rwanda—Drama. 2. Genocide—Drama.
3. Rwanda—Drama. I. Title.

PS3618.O463O94 2007
812'.6—dc22

2007020535

Designed by Cassandra J. Pappas

www.fsgbooks.com

1 3 5 7 9 10 8 6 4 2

For my son,
Henry Rogers

Contents

Acknowledgments

I wish to thank the following organizations and people in both the United States and Rwanda who were instrumental in the development of the play, whether through their support, creative input, professional advice, or editorial criticism: the NEA/TCG Theatre Residency Program for Playwrights; all of the artists and staff at the Salt Lake Acting Company, especially Nancy Borgenicht, Allen Nevins, David Kirk Chambers, and David Mong; Professor Howard Lehman of the University of Utah; Paul Meshejian and Michele Volansky and everyone at the PlayPenn new play development conference, with special thanks to my cast and director, Lucie Tiberghien; David Rogers; Susan Spencer Smith; Dr. Eric Helland; John Buzzetti; Raymond Simba; Adelit Rukomangana; and Helen Vesperini and Jean-Pierre Sagahutu.

In London, I am grateful to those whose support or creative input was instrumental in the play's completion: Nicholas Hynter, Tim Levy, and everyone at the National Theatre; Out of Joint; Jessica Swale; the original cast of Jude Akuwudike, William Armstrong, Babou Ceesay, Chipo Chung, Nick Fletcher, Andrew Garfield, Matthew Marsh, Tanya Moodie, Lucian Msamati, Adura Onashile, and Danny Sapani; and, most emphatically, Max Stafford-Clark.

Finally, I wish to express my gratitude to Rebecca Ashley, who has been involved with this play since its inception. Without her counsel and encouragement, it simply would not exist.

J. T. ROGERS
May 2007

The Overwhelming was originally developed in the United States at the Salt Lake Acting Company with support from the NEA/TCG Theatre Residency Program for Playwrights. The play was further developed with the support of PlayPenn.

Production History

The Overwhelming was originally produced at the National Theatre's Cottesloe Theatre in association with Out of Joint in London on May 9, 2006.

Director: Max Stafford-Clark. Designer: Tim Shortall. Lighting designer: Johanna Town. Sound designer: Gareth Fry. Assistant director: Jessica Swale. Dialect coaches: Jean-Pierre Blanchard, Mary Blewitt, Kate Godfrey, and Gabo Wilson. Production managers: Laurence Holderness and Gary Beestone. Stage manager: David Milling. Deputy stage manager: Sharon Hobden. Assistant stage managers: Ali Biggs and Harry Guthrie. Costume supervisor: Caroline Waterman. Associate sound designer: Carolyn Downing. Assistant to designer: Jason Southgate. Assistant to lighting designer: Nathan Seabrook. Design associate: Alan Bain. Assistant production manager: James Manley. Production photographer: John Haynes.

CHARLES WOOLSEY,
a U.S. embassy official . . . . William Armstrong

JACK EXLEY . . . . Matthew Marsh

JOSEPH GASANA . . . . Jude Akuwudike

JEAN-CLAUDE BUISSON,
a French diplomat . . . . Nick Fletcher

LINDA WHITE-KEELER,
Jack's wife . . . . Tanya Moodie

GEOFFREY EXLEY,
Jack's son . . . . Andrew Garfield

SAMUEL MIZINGA,
a Rwandan government official . . . . Danny Sapani

RWANDAN MAN,
a politician . . . . Lucian Msamati

RWANDAN DOCTOR . . . . Chipo Chung

GÉRARD,
the Exley family's servant . . . . Babou Ceesay

BRITISH RED CROSS DOCTOR . . . . William Armstrong

MARKET WOMAN . . . . Adura Onashile

MARKET MAN . . . . Lucian Msamati

JAN VERBEEK,
South African NGO worker . . . . Nick Fletcher

ELISE KAYITESI,
Joseph's wife . . . . Chipo Chung

POLICEMAN . . . . Lucian Msamati

WOMAN IN CLUB . . . . Adura Onashile

MAN IN CLUB . . . . Lucian Msamati

UN MAJOR . . . . Lucian Msamati

Other parts played by members of the Company

The Overwhelming had its U.S. premiere at the Roundabout Theatre Company's Laura Pels Theatre in New York City on October 23, 2007.

Director: Max Stafford-Clark. Production stage manager: Pat Sosnow. Set designer: Tim Shortall. Costume designer: Tobin Ost. Lighting designer: David Weiner. Sound designer: Gareth Fry.

CHARLES WOOLSEY,
a U.S. embassy official . . . . James Rebhorn

JACK EXLEY . . . . Sam Robards

JOSEPH GASANA . . . . Ron Cephas Jones

JEAN-CLAUDE BUISSON,
a French diplomat . . . . Boris McGiver

LINDA WHITE-KEELER,
Jack's wife . . . . Linda Powell

GEOFFREY EXLEY,
Jack's son . . . . Michael Stahl-David

SAMUEL MIZINGA,
a Rwandan government official . . . . Charles Parnell

RWANDAN MAN,
a politician . . . . Owiso Odera

RWANDAN DOCTOR . . . . Sharon Washington

GÉRARD,
the Exley family's servant . . . . Chris Chalk

BRITISH RED CROSS DOCTOR . . . . James Rebhorn

MARKET WOMAN . . . . Tisola Logan

MARKET MAN . . . . Owiso Odera

JAN VERBEEK,
a South African NGO worker . . . . Boris McGiver

ELISE KAYITESI,
Joseph's wife . . . . Sharon Washington

POLICEMAN . . . . Owiso Odera

WOMAN IN CLUB . . . . Tisola Logan

MAN IN CLUB . . . . Owiso Odera

UN MAJOR . . . . Owiso Odera

Other parts played by members of the Company

The Overwhelming

Think—
When you speak of our weaknesses,
Also of the dark time
That brought them forth.

—BERTOLT BRECHT,
from "After the Flood"

NOTES ON LANGUAGE AND STAGING

The use of a slash at the beginning or in the middle of a line of dialogue indicates that the next line of dialogue begins at that moment—creating verbal overlap.

A sentence ending with ". . ." indicates that the speaker has trailed off. A sentence ending with "—" indicates that the speaker is cut off midsentence.

French and Kinyarwanda, the two main languages of Rwanda, are spoken throughout the play. Sometimes the audience is to understand what is being said, sometimes not. When the Rwandan characters speak English, they do so with French-African accents.

Scene numbers are used only to delineate a change in location. The play flies along without stopping for breath—each scene shifting into the next without pause.

CHARACTERS

The American family

JACK EXLEY
GEOFFREY EXLEY (his son)
LINDA WHITE-KEELER (his wife)

Other foreigners

CHARLES WOOLSEY (U.S. embassy official)
JEAN-CLAUDE BUISSON (French diplomat)
BRITISH DOCTOR (for the International Red Cross)
JAN VERBEEK (South African NGO worker)
UN MAJOR (a Bangladeshi)

The Rwandans

JOSEPH GASANA
also plays Waiters, Hospital Orderlies, and Servant
ELISE KAYITESI (his wife)
also plays Party Guest and Rwandan doctor
SAMUEL MIZINGA (Rwandan government official)
GÉRARD (the Exley family's servant)
also plays Party Guest

MAN AT FRENCH EMBASSY PARTY

also plays Market Man, Policeman, and Man in Club

WOMAN IN CLUB

also plays Party Waitress and Market Woman

The play is performed with a cast of eleven.

Three actors—two white men and one black woman—play the Exley family.

Two white actors play Woolsey/British Doctor and Buisson/Verbeek, respectively.

One black actor plays the UN Major and the Man at Embassy Party and his secondary roles.

Five black actors play Joseph, Elise, Mizinga, Gérard, Woman in Club, and their secondary roles.

SETTING

Kigali, Rwanda, early 1994.

In the late nineteenth century, the Belgian King Leopold II launched a campaign to conquer the Congo basin of Africa. Over the following decades, through conquest and then subjugation, millions of Congolese were killed. The word in the Mongo language for this onslaught was lokeli, *or "the overwhelming."*

Act One

SCENE 1

(Friday afternoon. A torrential downpour. Two white Americans, JACK, *forties, and* WOOLSEY, *a little older, are in a car.* WOOLSEY *is driving. Their conversation is interrupted by a deafening crack of thunder. They shout to be heard over the storm.)*

WOOLSEY: Don't worry! / These are the best roads in Africa!

JACK: I'm fine! Really! Thank you!

WOOLSEY: Water's a different story. Don't ever drink from the tap, whatever people tell you. / That goes for teethbrushing, too. If you didn't boil it or unscrew it, don't drink it!

JACK: I know! I've done a lot of traveling!

WOOLSEY: You ever had serious diarrhea?

JACK: . . . I'm not sure!

WOOLSEY: How long you here?

JACK: Just the semester!

WOOLSEY: Well, get ready for it! For the next four months, when you fart, you'll fart with fear!

(The rain has stopped, almost instantaneously. The sun comes out. JACK *looks around as* WOOLSEY *stares straight ahead.)*

JACK: God, that's incredible! / I've been all over the world, but that is . . .

WOOLSEY: Flick of a switch turns it on, flick of a switch turns it off.

JACK: Amazing.

WOOLSEY: Yes, indeed.

(They drive for a moment. Then, leaping back in where they left off . . .)

JACK: Brezhnev!

WOOLSEY: Perfect example!

JACK: God, I'd forgotten / about him, too.

WOOLSEY: Exactly my point. Like it never happened.

JACK: Absolutely right.

WOOLSEY: Forty years. / God knows how much money and blood.

JACK: Incredible. Just incredible.

WOOLSEY: Berlin Wall's down, what, four years? Already ancient history.

JACK: I don't think my son even knows who Brezhnev was.

WOOLSEY: There's no enemy now. We won. And yet I miss those fuckers. No, I do. I'm old-school, Jack. I can say "Do you want to defect?" and "How much for the entire night?" in ten languages. There's nothing to push against. We're just going through the motions. Four years I've been here, shuffling papers, picking up tourists at the airport. Why? No one can tell me. What are we protecting? No one can tell me. I don't know, Washington doesn't know, you don't know—*do* you know?

JACK: You mean—

WOOLSEY: Yeah. Tell me.

JACK: I . . . No, I don't—

WOOLSEY: Come on, Jack. Give me a fresh perspective. We're still strangers; we can say anything.

JACK *(laughing)*: Two hours in Kigali and you want my thoughts? I teach international relations / not mind read— What?

WOOLSEY: Exactly. *(Off the word "What?")* "International relations." With whom? Who are we relating with? Four years, I still haven't gotten an answer. You find an answer, you let me know.

JACK: You'll be the first.

WOOLSEY: Anything, really. You find out anything interesting. People. Places. Happenings. You let me know first. Will you do that?

JACK: Sure I can. I'm just visiting.

WOOLSEY: Me, too.

JACK: I just know one person here.

WOOLSEY: That'll change. You like good beer?

JACK: Sure.

WOOLSEY: The beer here tastes like piss. Makes you thirsty for Schlitz. God, what I wouldn't give for an ice-cold Schlitz. Let's swing by UNAMIR before we go to the hotel, see if we can score some Ghanaian stuff.

JACK: The Ghanaians make good beer?

WOOLSEY: Geniuses with beer. This is a fucked-up continent, but the Ghanaians, they're doing all right. You wanna go by the embassy and check in first?

JACK: Why?

WOOLSEY: Why? Why, in a country where people are getting assassinated left and right, would you want the United States government to know where you are and how to get in touch with you?

JACK: But the Accords are—

WOOLSEY: What about them?

JACK: There's a cease-fire. There's no fighting.

WOOLSEY: And you know this how?

JACK: From . . . everywhere. The BBC, / African news sources. The guerrillas agreed to—the RPF laid down their arms. I contacted people at the UN before coming. They told me things were . . .

WOOLSEY: Oh, well, "the BBC" . . . *(Off the word "UN.")* Ho-ho! Sweet Jesus.

JACK: Are you telling me something different? My family's arriving tomorrow—

WOOLSEY: Don't worry. They'll be fine. You'll be fine.

JACK: I'm here for research.

WOOLSEY: Good.

JACK: I'm just writing a book.

WOOLSEY: Good.

JACK: I wanted to come here.

WOOLSEY: Sure.

(They drive in silence, looking straight ahead. Then:)

WOOLSEY: Oh. And happy New Year.

SCENE 2

(A pool of light reveals JOSEPH.*)*

JOSEPH: Dear Jack, I hope this finds you well. I am sorry to report that I will be unable to meet you at the airport. If I had any choice in the matter, you know I would be there to greet you, my friend. But I will see you after the weekend, first thing Monday morning at my office. It was an unexpected surprise to read that you have changed your plans and are now bringing your family. But it is wise of you to come a day ahead and make sure everything is in order for them. You have always been cautious, Jack. Here you will find this trait very useful. Unfortunately, the housing I arranged is now no longer adequate, but we will find you something else.

Again, I am so sorry to hear about Carol. This must be a very difficult time for your son. As you say, coming here is not Geoffrey's choice, but I know you will take good care of him.

SCENE 3

(Later that day, WOOLSEY *and* JACK, *glasses of beer in hand, sit at a table by the pool of the Hôtel des Mille Collines. Jack is in mid–enthusiastic speech.)*

JACK: I would love Geoffrey to have that kind of experience. Like I did when I was his age.

WOOLSEY: So you've been to Africa before?

JACK: No, no. Sweden. Semester abroad. But even that gives you a sense of being the foreign—the, the "other." And since then—Look, through my work, I've done village-level research in Indonesia, Peru. Had the kind of firsthand encounters where you experience—viscerally—life as the outsider. There's an empathy that comes from that. I want him to have that while he's still young enough for it to make a difference. Instill a sense of humility and—yes!—of questioning. God! I don't want to raise another American who doesn't question. I see them in my classes: eighteen years old, this sense of entitlement. The scope of what they take for granted!

WOOLSEY: So you want to take things away from him.

JACK: No. I mean . . . well . . .

WOOLSEY: Temporarily.

JACK: Yes.

WOOLSEY: For his own good.

JACK: Exactly.

WOOLSEY: Well, you've come to the right place for that. If the world were flat, this would be the edge. And you chose to— You're obviously having a good time, I don't want to be the / drunken expat who—

JACK: No, no. Please. Tell me what you think of this place. Really.

(A WAITER *enters and replaces the empty bottles with fresh ones.)*

WOOLSEY *(to the* WAITER*)*: Tu veux me soûler, de nouveau, huh? *(Trying to get me drunk again, are you?)*

WAITER: Mais bien sûr, monsieur, à quoi est-ce que je sers sinon? *(But of course, sir, why else am I here?)*

(They both laugh, then, as the WAITER *walks away . . .)*

WOOLSEY: He's dead.

JACK: . . . What?

WOOLSEY *(gestures off toward the* WAITER*)*: His wife was killed last week. Abducted. Raped. Cut up. Someone thought she was an RPF accomplice. They'll come for him. Matter of time.

JACK: Who?

WOOLSEY: Well, that's the million-dollar question, isn't it?

JACK: Why doesn't he—

WOOLSEY: Run? Go to the police? This isn't Sweden, Jack.

JACK: . . . How do you know this?

WOOLSEY *(takes a swig of his beer)*: I live here.

SCENE 4

(JOSEPH *appears again in his light.*)

JOSEPH: In late January you will have missed most of the rainy season, and you will find the weather beautiful when you arrive. You must take your family to the Nyungwe Forest while you are here. Bring your tourist dollars so you can buy some ugly trinkets you will never use. Speaking of this, would you please bring me two Michael Jordan T-shirts, size small, in black. This will make me a very popular man.

I am amazed sometimes how little I miss from the States. Except the toilet paper. Just kidding. I cannot wait to begin our work together, Jack. What a pleasure it will be, my friend, to share my country with you.

SCENE 5

(*A cocktail reception at the French embassy the following evening. A Rwandan* WAITER *and* WAITRESS *silently pass food and drink to* PARTY GUESTS. *Near the back of the room is a well-dressed Rwandan* MAN, *standing alone.* JACK *and* WOOLSEY *stand together, drinks in hand. Nearby,* LINDA, *a black American in her early thirties, is talking to* BUISSON, *a French government official in his thirties. With them is* GEOFFREY, *a white American, seventeen. He is less than happy to be here.*)

BUISSON: No, I'm positive. I've seen your photo before.

LINDA: Well, it could be. I'm—

GEOFFREY: Denim jacket, hair up in a bun?

BUISSON: Yes!

GEOFFREY: It's the dust-jacket shot everyone remembers.

BUISSON: Ah, you are a writer!

LINDA: I'm impressed you've even seen / one of . . .

BUISSON: Are you a poet?

LINDA: No.

BUISSON: Novels, then.

LINDA: Not yet.

BUISSON: This is like a game . . . Histories of— No, no, don't tell me . . . Black America! Histories of Black America!

GEOFFREY: She does creative nonfiction.

BUISSON: I'm sorry?

LINDA: Personal essays. Narratives of self.

BUISSON: Ah! Like Montaigne.

LINDA: Yes!

BUISSON: What was it Nietzsche said: "Truly, that such a man has written adds to the joy of life."

LINDA: I couldn't agree more. Montaigne is without peer.

BUISSON: I have read everything of his. If one is French—well, if one is French, and in my profession, one must.

GEOFFREY: "Living on this earth."

BUISSON: I'm sorry?

GEOFFREY: The quote. It's "adds to the joy of living on this earth." From *Birth of Tragedy.*

BUISSON: And do you speak German, Geoffrey?

GEOFFREY: . . . Uh, no.

BUISSON: So you are correcting me with a translation.

LINDA *(trying to save the boy)*: Geoffrey's father and I were just telling him, next year at college he should *take* German. That's what Jack / studied in . . .

BUISSON *(staring straight at* GEOFFREY*)*: You see, this is the hazard of translation. An idea is written down. Another man is drawn to it. His mission, to spread this thought deeper into the world. But there is a difference between having words and understanding their meaning.

JACK *(gesturing for him)*: Geoffrey!

(Eagerly taking his "out," GEOFFREY *mumbles a good-bye under his breath as he heads toward* JACK *and* WOOLSEY.*)*

BUISSON *(turning to* LINDA*)*: What is so often missing is context. And as we diplomats know, not having context is a dangerous thing.

*(*BUISSON *kisses* LINDA*'s hand and crosses to the Rwandan* MAN, *as* GEOFFREY *has joined* JACK *and* WOOLSEY.*)*

WOOLSEY: So what are you, high school? Eleventh? Twelfth?

GEOFFREY: Twelfth.

JACK *(to* WOOLSEY*)*: Very good, Chuck.

*(*LINDA *flags down the* WAITRESS *for a refill.* BUISSON *and the Rwandan* MAN *speak together as* MIZINGA, *another Rwandan man, in his late thirties and equally well dressed, enters the room.)*

WOOLSEY: I've got two sons. All grown up now.

JACK: Really!

WOOLSEY: Graduated. Jobs. One's already having a baby.

JACK: Your work's done, then.

WOOLSEY: My father told me, "When you pay the down payments on their first mortgages, then you're done." So, Geoff—

JACK: Actually, / he prefers—

GEOFFREY: I can tell him, Dad. *(To* WOOLSEY.*)* Geoffrey.

*(*MIZINGA *has joined* BUISSON *and the other Rwandan* MAN *in conversation.)*

WOOLSEY: You play sports, Geoffrey?

GEOFFREY: No.

WOOLSEY: Foreign language?

GEOFFREY: No.

JACK: Geoffrey. *(To* WOOLSEY.*)* He's fantastic at languages. Just like his mother.

WOOLSEY: Really? Linda told me she couldn't speak a word of—

GEOFFREY: She's not my mother. You know: kinda obvious.

JACK: I mean my first wife. Carol.

WOOLSEY: Carol.

JACK: Yes, Geoff's— I mean . . . *(To* GEOFFREY.*)* Sorry . . . *(To* WOOLSEY.*)* Geoffrey's / mother.

WOOLSEY: Carol.

JACK: Yes.

WOOLSEY: Carol wasn't in your file, Jack.

JACK: Oh. Well. She and I . . . divorced years ago.

GEOFFREY: *Three* years ago.

JACK: Well, okay! Who'd like another drink?

(As JACK *goes to get refills,* LINDA *is approached by* MIZINGA.*)*

MIZINGA: Bonsoir, madame, c'est un plaisir de faire votre connaissance. *(Good evening, madam. It's enchanting to make your acquaintance.)*

LINDA: Forgive me. I don't speak French.

MIZINGA *(switching to English)*: Ah! You are *noire Américaine.* Forgive *me.* I mistook you for someone else, equally beautiful.

LINDA: Sorry to disappoint.

MIZINGA: Samuel Mizinga.

LINDA: Linda White-Keeler.

MIZINGA: I'm sorry?

LINDA *(a little slowly)*: Linda White-Keeler.

MIZINGA: This is an American name?

LINDA: My mother's name is White, and my father's—

MIZINGA: Ah! "White" *and* "Keeler." Of course. You said "White-Keeler," and I thought—

(He draws his thumb across his throat as WOOLSEY *drifts over to them.)*

WOOLSEY: Linda, Sam's in the government. One of the ones with all his marbles.

LINDA: Really?

MIZINGA: Simply serving my country.

WOOLSEY: He's working on the BBTG.

LINDA: The . . . ?

WOOLSEY: Sorry. *(To* MIZINGA.*)* She's fresh off the plane. *(To* LINDA.*)* Broad-based transitional government. Now that the shooting's stopped.

MIZINGA: And how is the golf coming, Charles?

WOOLSEY: Same old, same old.

MIZINGA: Mr. Woolsey is famous here for how far he can hack the ball. But his putting *(as he mimes doing so)* is a painful thing.

WOOLSEY: Thank you, Sam. Always good to be loved.

MIZINGA: We all play with him, of course. After all, what man does not like to win?

WOOLSEY *(as he moves back toward* GEOFFREY*)*: Happy New Year, Sam.

MIZINGA: And you, Charles.

(As WOOLSEY *and* BUISSON *cross paths . . .)*

BUISSON *(extending his hand)*: Bonsoir. Vous serez toujours le bienvenu chez nous. *(Good evening. You will always be welcome here.)*

WOOLSEY *(brushing past)*: Great.

MIZINGA *(to* LINDA*)*: I am told you are a writer.

LINDA: That got around quick.

MIZINGA: I confess, reading is my weakness. Balzac is my favorite. I have read most of him.

LINDA: Really.

MIZINGA: The sweep of his work. That one man could capture an entire people. Quite magnificent. Perhaps you will write about us.

LINDA: Yes! That's— I mean, I'm here to . . . Sorry. Half my brain is still in the States. Yesterday I was in two feet of snow and a down parka. I'm still adjusting to being here in paradise. I hope that's not offensive.

MIZINGA: Yes, terribly offensive. I shall have to have you shot. *(Pause.)* That was a joke.

LINDA: Ah! When my husband's son and I flew in today, the mountains were—

MIZINGA: Like the Alps, people say.

LINDA: Yes!

MIZINGA: Rwanda is called the Switzerland of Africa. Or perhaps it should be the other way around. I think you will find we are like the Swiss. Organized, efficient. People take orders here very well. This is why it is so important.

LINDA: What is?

MIZINGA: That our leaders have the best interests of this country at heart. There are many of us here who are working very hard to make sure this is the case. We cannot afford to go backward.

*(*JACK *returns to* WOOLSEY *and* GEOFFREY, *drinks in hand.)*

WOOLSEY: So, Geoffrey, what *do* you do? Twelfth grade, the world wide open.

GEOFFREY: Study.

JACK: Geoffrey's actually the district champ in extemporaneous speaking. It's where you draw three topics from a hat. You pick one—global warming, race relations—you get five minutes to prepare. Then you try to persuade the judges to your point of view. Geoffrey came in first this year. The entire school district.

WOOLSEY: What did you speak on?

GEOFFREY: Organic farming.

WOOLSEY: You won with a speech on organic farming?

GEOFFREY: Yeah.

WOOLSEY: Sort of a "Mother Earth good, pesticides bad" kind of a thing?

GEOFFREY: Sure.

WOOLSEY: Your parents and Linda must be very proud.

GEOFFREY: Thanks.

WOOLSEY: Terse is good. Terse will get you far in life. Look at me. I ask too many questions. I got sent here.

(LINDA *and* MIZINGA, *in midconversation.)*

LINDA: Essays, about my personal experience here.

MIZINGA: To convey this to American readers?

LINDA: Yes! It's a much larger magazine than those I usually— So I'm thrilled. And intimidated.

MIZINGA: I am sure your work is excellent.

LINDA: No. Thank you, but what I mean is, being here, for the first time . . . From what I've learned, I have ancestors from the Great Lakes region. They were taken from here in chains. I'm *from* here.

MIZINGA: Then you must feel a bond with—

LINDA: A responsibility. I don't want to be another tourist waxing lyrical about "Mother Africa." I want to really see this place. Ask hard questions. Write something that opens eyes and instills an interest. And now I'm hearing myself, and I sound like some / sort of . . .

MIZINGA: You are being honest. And for that, I thank you. I hope you will allow me to be of service. To your writing.

LINDA: That would be . . . thank you. Yes.

SCENE 6

(JOSEPH *appears again in his light.)*

JOSEPH: You will find Kigali a clean city. And safe. Even for Linda. This is not a city where your wife will be afraid to be out at night, like Paris or Milwaukee. Now that she is coming, I am eager to meet her. From your letters, she sounds like a handful. And you have always liked your hands very full, Jack. Congratulations.

Forgive me, my friend, for urging you to come on such short notice. But when one has a window, one must open it. Your coming now allows us to help each other. And we must help our friends, Jack. Always.

SCENE 7

(The end of the party at the French embassy, many drinks consumed. The WAITER *and* WAITRESS, *as well as the other* PARTY GUESTS, *are gone.* LINDA, WOOLSEY, BUISSON, MIZINGA, *and the other well-dressed Rwandan* MAN *are listening to* JACK. GEOFFREY *sits to the side, watching.)*

JACK: History is this all-powerful, irreducible monolith. This is what we're taught.

(MIZINGA *translates into French for the* MAN, *who stands next to him.)*

MIZINGA: L'histoire est une chose toute puissante, monolithique. / Voilà ce qu'on nous enseigne. *(We are taught that history is powerful. It is a monolith.)*

JACK: A series of events, outside our control. / This torrent, pouring forth, sweeping all of us inexorably forward.

MIZINGA: Il dit que nous sommes tous dans les mains du destin. *(He says we are all in the hands of fate.)*

WOOLSEY: You're saying that's bullshit.

JACK: Exactly! Utter bullshit!

MIZINGA: Mais l'autre / dit c'est n'importe quoi. *(That one says you are speaking bullshit.)*

LINDA: We were in Cuzco when Jack got the idea for the book.

JACK: This Dutch couple, running our hotel. Younger than us. *(To* LINDA.*)* Well, than me.

LINDA: This was in Peru, up in the mountains. On our honeymoon.

(They are "on," telling the story together, not for the first time.)

JACK: They'd adopted twelve boys, just the two of them. / Kids from the slums.

LINDA: They did this on their own. They told us there was no plan. / It just happened.

JACK: They saw all these other children, so they started taking donations / from their guests.

LINDA: From people like us, just passing through.

JACK: They feed five hundred children daily.

LINDA: You saw what they were doing, you had to get involved.

JACK: These people aren't being swept along, they're doing the sweeping.

LINDA: And this is when Jack . . . *(She gestures to him to "take it away.")*

JACK: And the question hits me: What's the connection? Between this couple and people all over the world, affecting change—true change—underneath the radar.

MIZINGA *(continuing to translate)*: Il dit qu'il y a des gens qui, à eux seuls, sont vraiment capables de changer les choses. / Qu'ont-ils en commun? *(He says there are people in the world who truly change things, all on their own. / So how are they connected to each other?)*

LINDA: When I took Jack's class, he had us all in the palm of his hand. He'd start talking, and I'd just—

JACK: In international relations, you find your question by finding the right lens to look through. Then you seek your answers through creating cross-national models of comparative—

LINDA: Jargon alert!

JACK *(gestures "thank you" to* LINDA*)*: You collect examples. In this case, individuals. That couple in Cuzco, I started with them. Then a tribal chief I interviewed in Borneo, fighting his government over deforestation. One man!

BUISSON: And the book you are writing, it is about these sort of people?

JACK: Exactly! A comparative analysis of grassroots activists around the world, standing up for what is right. What's the common variable? Personality? Class? Culture? What can we extrapolate from these people who act, even in the face of the impossible?

MAN: Vous avez beaucoup de chances. Ici on n'a pas ce genre de personne.

MIZINGA *(translating)*: "You are fortunate. Here we do not have these sort of people."

JACK: You do! The heart of my book is about a doctor here in Kigali. I'm here to write about the work he's doing: one man in one hospital, under the radar. People like this are changing history. / This is what . . .

MIZINGA *(translating)*: Ce livre il s'agit d'un médecin ici à Kigali. *(He is here for a book about a doctor in Kigali.)*

JACK: A book about him. About what he and so many others are accomplishing. Not just another footnoted tome that molds away in a bunch of university libraries, but something that speaks to the world at large. That galvanizes the— *(To* MIZINGA.*)* Forgive me, / I'm monopolizing the . . .

MIZINGA: Please. Your passion is invigorating.

JACK: People *do* take action.

MIZINGA: But not every person here who takes action is to be trusted. You must / learn this.

JACK: Of course. What I'm saying is that individuals make a difference.

MIZINGA: This is in America?

JACK: No! Everywhere!

MAN: Les gens qui peuvent changer l'histoire? Ils sont partout? Je vous en trouverais moi a Butare? *(These people are "everywhere"? People who can "change history"? I am to find them in Butare?)*

JACK: Look, this isn't just another theoretical humanist argument. There are concrete examples. People we all know. Look at the Philippines! *(Snaps his fingers.)* What's his, what's / his . . .

LINDA: Benigno Aquino.

JACK *(to her)*: This is why I love you. *(To his "audience.")* Two heart attacks in solitary confinement, exiled to the States, barely able to walk, but still protesting the Marcos regime. Speaking out, setting an example, one man!

WOOLSEY: And they shot him.

(Everyone turns and looks at WOOLSEY.*)*

WOOLSEY: Aquino finally flew back, he got off the plane in Manila, and they shot him.

(Everyone turns and looks at JACK.*)*

JACK *(pause)*: Okay, yes. But my point is—

LINDA: His wife.

JACK: Thank you!

LINDA: Corazon Aquino stepped into her husband's shoes, Marcos fell, she became president.

JACK: A housewife! No political experience, training, interest. History crashes down on her head, and what does she do? She acts! The housewife moves the monolith.

MAN: Mais ici, nous sommes au Rwanda.

MIZINGA *(translating)*: "But this is Rwanda."

MAN: Nous n'avons pas d'Aquino.

MIZINGA: "We have no Aquino."

MAN: Nous n'avons pas de Mandela ou de Jefferson.

MIZINGA: "We have no Mandela or Thomas Jefferson."

MAN: Sans les / hommes de cette envergure, l'histoire ne peut pas changer. Ce qui doit arriver arrivera.

JACK *(to the* MAN*)*: I'm sorry, I don't / believe we've . . .

LINDA: Jack, let him finish.

MIZINGA *(off* MAN*'s "envergure")*: "Without men like that, history cannot be changed. What is to happen here will happen."

JACK *(to the* MAN*)*: No. I'm sorry, but no. The world is not dictated by Kaiser Geschichte. You / have to . . .

LINDA: Honey, / you're—

JACK *(to* LINDA*)*: I know! *(Back to the* MAN.*)* Forgive me. I know I'm your guest, but— Look, Mandela, Jefferson: Their impact can't be denied. But glorifying a handful of great individuals releases *us* from responsibility. That couple in Cuzco; this doctor here; you, me: We're the ones who have to be willing to stand up and make a difference. This is how history moves forward. One pebble redirects the river!

BUISSON: But what if the river becomes an ocean?

LINDA: Then you get more pebbles.

BUISSON: How pretty that sounds, but / it is not a realistic . . .

LINDA: What's the alternative? "It's not my problem"? / That's your paradigm for dealing with the world?

MIZINGA *(to* WOOLSEY*)*: He must understand, Charles, we are still a nation in shock. *(To* JACK.*) Inkoytanyi* terrorists have invaded this country, slaughtered our citizens. The UN is here now, and things are quiet, but we have been victims of terrible crimes. We are not ready for what you are speaking about.

LINDA: But the Arusha Accords are / in place, everything is . . .

MAN *(growing agitated)*: Ce pays est encore infesté d'espions et de meutriers. / Les Hutus se battent pour leur survie. Notre pays est au bord de la destruction. Nous sommes des ésclaves de l'histoire. Ne devons faire tout ce qui est en notre pouvoir pour survivre.

MIZINGA *(translating)*: "Spies and murderers are still among us. The real Rwandans are fighting for their survival"—I am only translating, you understand—"we are holding on to our country by our fingernails. We are trapped by our history. / We must do what we can to survive."

JACK: No, no! I'm sorry, but that's completely fatalistic. I'm not saying to stand up isn't hard. Terribly hard. But look at the world. Look at your country! This endless cycle of ethnic killings—the level of bloodshed. You have to go beyond this! The wheel of history pushed forward by your shoulders! For God's sake, what's the alternative?

(The MAN *speaks to* JACK *in Kinyarwanda, his voice rising. Words hard, sharp.)*

MAN: Uratekereza ko har' ikintu twahindura nizi nyenzi zose zishaka gutwara ubutaka bwacu? Kwica abana bacu? Reb' ibyo barigukorera bagenzi bacu b'aBarundi! Amaraso zameneka, mbere yuko undi mwami ategeka iki gihugu! Ingufuz'abahutu zizatuma! Urwanda rutagwa mu maboko y'Abanyamahanga! Tuzuzuz' amaliba n'amaraso yabo hanyuma tuboherez' iwabo muli Ethiopia! Urumva? Tuzabatema bose! Ntabwo tuzongera kub'abaja!*

(The MAN *exits. Everyone turns to* MIZINGA.*)*

MIZINGA *(with a smile)*: He says, "Welcome to Rwanda."

SCENE 8

(Late that night, GEOFFREY*'s hotel room.* GEOFFREY *stands with towel and toothbrush.* JACK *stands in the doorway. They stare at each other.)*

JACK: Hi.

GEOFFREY: Hey.

(Silence.)

JACK: If you need any help, anytime, with any of your coursework, Linda or I can—

GEOFFREY: Thanks. I'll let you know.

JACK: I know this wasn't exactly how you expected to spend the last semester of your senior year.

*You think we can change things here with these filthy cockroaches all around us? Plotting to take our land? Kill our children? Look what they are doing to our brothers and sisters in Burundi! The streets will run with blood before another Tutsi king rules this country! Hutu Power will save Rwanda from these foreign devils! We will fill the rivers with bodies and send them all back to Ethiopia! Do you hear me? We will cut them, every one! We will not be slaves again!

GEOFFREY: Things happen.

(They stare at each other.)

JACK: Yes. They do.

*(*JACK *turns to leave, then turns back.)*

JACK: Do you . . . do you remember when we went to Bali? We took that boat and went to that isolated island?

GEOFFREY: I was five. Who remembers things from when / they're five.

JACK: Right. Of course. Your mother and I, we took you there. For a week we did nothing. The stillness was . . . We stayed in this hut. The three of us. No electricity. We'd fish out of the sea, cook it right on the beach. You'd eat all of yours, then half of mine. "Your shoulders are down." You kept saying that to me. "You're so relaxed, Daddy, your shoulders are down." You sure you don't . . . ?

*(*GEOFFREY *is still, watching him.)*

JACK: For your mother and me, it was . . . transforming. To be so removed. Really see yourself. That kind of clarity can change you. Make things different. I want us to have that, Geoffrey. Here. The three of us. I know you and Linda barely . . . It's difficult for her, too. She never expected— You'll see. You'll get to know her. You'll understand why . . . I know you and I haven't spent a lot of . . . I'm so glad you're here.

(They stare at each other.)

GEOFFREY: Good night, Dad.

SCENE 9

(Monday morning, an office at Kigali Central Hospital. JACK *is meeting with a female* RWANDAN DOCTOR*. A Rwandan* ORDERLY *is pouring a bottle of Fanta into a glass for* JACK*.)*

RWANDAN DOCTOR: And have you found accommodations?

JACK: My wife and son and I have been staying at the Mills Collins. *(To the* ORDERLY.*)* Merci.

(Done serving, the ORDERLY *steps away from them and stands unmoving.)*

RWANDAN DOCTOR: How did you come to choose the *Mille Collines*?

JACK: Oh. Thank you. We didn't have time to find a place here to rent before we came. So I decided, once we got here, I'd have to go around asking *(haltingly)*: Excusez moi, où pourrais-je trouver une maison à louer? *(Excuse me, where can I rent a house?)* I inexplicably took German in graduate school, so that's the extent of my French.

RWANDAN DOCTOR: But you used it.

JACK: I used all of it.

RWANDAN DOCTOR: And the effort is appreciated.

JACK: Well, I'm—we're—all thrilled to be here. My God, the flight in: breathtaking. The hills. So green. Endless.

RWANDAN DOCTOR: A thousand hills.

JACK: Exactly. That's the phrase in Kinyarwanda to describe your country, isn't it?

RWANDAN DOCTOR: I am impressed.

JACK: Well, one should know something about where / one is . . .

RWANDAN DOCTOR: Your country is named for Amerigo Vespucci, I believe.

JACK: Yes.

RWANDAN DOCTOR: An Italian.

JACK: That's right.

RWANDAN DOCTOR: Why don't you speak Italian in America? I have always wondered this.

JACK: Well, he discovered, but he didn't—

RWANDAN DOCTOR: But he was there first.

JACK: No, Christopher Columbus was first. I think.

RWANDAN DOCTOR: Christopher Columbus was also an Italian.

JACK: That's true.

RWANDAN DOCTOR: Perhaps there is a conspiracy.

JACK: I'm beginning to think so.

RWANDAN DOCTOR: If you will forgive me, I would not stay long at the Mille Collines.

JACK: No, we've found a place / in Nyamirambo.

RWANDAN DOCTOR: I would move quickly from there.

JACK: . . . Okay. Is there . . . ?

RWANDAN DOCTOR: If I may be candid, your wife should not be seen at a place like that. To stay there, where women sell themselves to Western . . . We do not approve of this. We are not so carefree here. A home is much better. Someplace more private and safe. Safety is very important here.

(The DOCTOR *rises, and a surprised* JACK *does the same as the* ORDERLY *steps forward and whisks away* JACK*'s drink.)*

RWANDAN DOCTOR: It has been an honor to meet you. I hope your research is fruitful.

JACK: I'm sorry, there's been some sort of— I'm still waiting to see Dr. Gasana. Your secretary, I told her this.

RWANDAN DOCTOR: Gasana.

JACK: Yes. He's the subject of my book. Dr. Joseph Gasana. I'm here to see him.

RWANDAN DOCTOR: There is no Gasana here. We have no one by that name on our staff.

JACK: He's the specialist in— He runs your children's HIV clinic.

RWANDAN DOCTOR: Mr. Exley, how I dearly wish we had any specialists on our staff. We have no one by that name here.

JACK: That's not possible.

RWANDAN DOCTOR: But it is true.

JACK: This is where he works. This is his job.

RWANDAN DOCTOR: Someone has led you astray. I'm sorry. Please give your wife my best.

SCENE 10

(JOSEPH appears again.)

JOSEPH: Funding has become difficult of late. We are stretched far too thin. This is why I am so eager to begin our work, so that your book will call attention. And what we are doing so dearly needs attention. Ah! Perhaps you will even make me famous! Red carpets and cameras—pop, pop—everywhere I go! You see? You can take the man out of America, Jack, but once he has been, you can never take America out of the man.

I have missed you, my friend. There is no one here I can talk to like this. Your presence will be such a help, Jack. I count the days until your arrival.

SCENE 11

(The same morning. LINDA stands in the living room of a house. A young Rwandan MAN who looks to be in his early twenties stands across from her, suitcases at his feet. No one moves. Finally . . .)

LINDA: Thank you for bringing in the bags. That was very kind of you.

(The MAN smiles. He crosses to a chair and sits. LINDA stares at him. Silence.)

LINDA: Merci.

(The MAN *smiles but does not move. More silence.)*

LINDA: Merci beaucoup.

*(*GEOFFREY *enters from inside the house.)*

GEOFFREY: I'm going to take the / room in the back, if that's . . .

LINDA: Do you have any francs for the driver?

GEOFFREY: Uh, yeah, I—

LINDA: How much should we—

GEOFFREY: I don't know.

*(*GEOFFREY *takes out his wallet. He gives a bill to the* MAN, *who rises, takes it, and smiles.)*

MAN *(in Kinyarwanda)*: Urakoze. *(Thank you.)*

(The MAN *sits back down.* LINDA *and* GEOFFREY *look at each other.* GEOFFREY *hands another bill to the* MAN, *who again rises and takes it, with an even bigger smile.)*

MAN *(in Kinyarwanda)*: Murakoze cyane. *(Thank you very much.)*

(The MAN *sits back down. Silence. Finally . . .)*

LINDA: Monsieur—

(The phone rings. LINDA *crosses to it and picks it up.)*

LINDA *(into the phone)*: Allô, bonjour? . . . Oh, Mr. Mizinga!

(The MAN *stands up.)*

LINDA: Yes, we've just arrived. It's perfect. Thank you so much for finding us a . . . Oh . . . That's . . . Yes, we're free today . . . That would be lovely! . . . We'll see you then. And again, thank you so— *(She listens, then looks at the* MAN.*)* Yes . . . He's right here. *(Pause.)* I see . . . I see . . . *(Pause.)* Of course.

(She offers the phone to the MAN, *who crosses to her and takes it. He listens, then speaks into the phone.)*

MAN *(in Kinyarwanda)*: Yego bwana. Narihano ngutegereje nkuko wabyifuje bwana . . . Nibyo bwana . . . Ukubyifuza bwana . . .

Ndabyunva. *(Yes, sir. I was right here waiting, as you asked, sir . . . Of course, sir . . . Whatever you wish, sir . . . I understand.)*

(The MAN *hangs up the phone and starts to exit into the house. At the last moment, he turns back to them.)*

GÉRARD *(in Kinyarwanda)*: Murakaze bwana. Murakaze madami. Njyewe ndagiye. Mukomere kandi. *(Welcome, sir. Welcome, madam. You are both welcome. I will leave you now.)*

*(*GÉRARD *is gone.)*

LINDA *(to* GEOFFREY*)*: He works for us. His name's Gérard. He lives here.

SCENE 12

(That afternoon, the International Red Cross hospital. JACK *is meeting with a male* BRITISH DOCTOR. *Another Rwandan* ORDERLY, *thin and stooped, stands to the side.)*

BRITISH DOCTOR: Gasana.

JACK: Dr. Joseph Gasana. He's / the director of . . .

BRITISH DOCTOR: Yes! The children's HIV clinic at Kigali Central. / Clinical trials with antiretrovirals.

JACK: Exactly! Yes. So you know him.

BRITISH DOCTOR: Not personally, but I hear he's very good.

JACK: But they said he doesn't work there.

BRITISH DOCTOR: Welcome to Rwandan bureaucracy, Professor Exley.

JACK: They had no idea who I was even— How do you know my name?

BRITISH DOCTOR: Oh, everyone knows everyone here. Bit suffocating; wonderful for the gossip. Besides, it's not like we get a planeload of Americans every day, is it? Well, now the shooting's stopped, we do get a few. Visit the gorillas, visit the prostitutes; sort of a package tour. And by the way, condoms are an absolute must. With the prostitutes, that is. But didn't I just hear that the funding for your friend's clinic was cut off?

JACK: Joseph's?

BRITISH DOCTOR: Some sort of trouble with the authorities? *(He turns and speaks in French to the* ORDERLY.*)* Connaissez-vous un docteur du nom de Joseph Gasana? *(Do you know a Dr. Joseph Gasana?) (To* JACK.*)* You know him well?

JACK: Yes. He's one of my oldest friends.

BRITISH DOCTOR: C'est un pédiatre. Un specialiste de la prévention du Sida. Il travaille a l'autre hôpital. *(He's a pediatrician. A specialist in HIV prevention at the other hospital.)*

ORDERLY: Non, je suis désolé, Docteur, je ne connais pas de Dr. Gasana. *(I'm sorry, Doctor. I do not know a Dr. Joseph Gasana.)*

BRITISH DOCTOR *(to* JACK*)*: Are you sure he's not off at a conference or something?

JACK: No! He invited me. I got a letter from him just a week ago. He knows his work is the spine of my book. He's in Kigali. He has to be here.

BRITISH DOCTOR *(to the* ORDERLY*)*: Merci, François.

(The ORDERLY *nods and slowly shuffles out.)*

JACK: Are you sure he doesn't work here? Could he have transferred or—

BRITISH DOCTOR: I'm afraid we don't share staff with their hospital. And if you get sick, with all due respect, make sure you come here.

JACK *(gesturing toward where the* ORDERLY *left)*: Is he ill?

BRITISH DOCTOR: François? He's dying of AIDS.

JACK: Jesus.

BRITISH DOCTOR: Last of his family. Wife, six children, already gone. You want to talk about stoicism? These people, I'm in awe. Their grace, kindness. To maintain that in the face of AIDS, malaria, sleeping sickness—

JACK: You mean like—

BRITISH DOCTOR: Something medieval, yes. We've started to get reports from up north. Entire villages, just lying down, falling asleep, and dying.

JACK: God, I had no idea.

BRITISH DOCTOR: Why would you? You have to be here to start making sense of this place. Before I came, I read everything, thought I was a bloody expert. Then I got off the plane. Some things, though, still mystify. Country's organized on a ten-cell model.

JACK: Like the Tanzanian system that / Nyerere . . .

BRITISH DOCTOR: Precisely. It's divided into ten *préfectures*; tens all the way down to the neighborhood level. Organizational genius. So why do I see people here every day who are dying because they don't know about medicines that are readily available? What's this vaunted network being saved for? Because if the people running this country ever wanted to do something big, it would happen *(snaps his fingers)* like that. Perhaps he left, your friend.

JACK: Why would he do that?

BRITISH DOCTOR: Well, he's Tutsi, isn't he? Right now, if I were a Tutsi? Christ, I wouldn't stay here.

SCENE 13

(JOSEPH *stands in his light once again.)*

JOSEPH: What I see every day, it can be overwhelming. One's faith is tested, Jack. Daily. But what can I do but keep going? Educate the mothers and fathers, see my patients . . . Most of those I see are too young to even know the word. And how wrong that children should even be patients. With the limited medicines we have, I save those I can, pray for those I cannot, and think always of Benjamin Franklin. Do you remember that class we took so long ago? I still take my history seriously, Jack. I am *Rwandais*, after all. Do you remember what he said? "The definition of insanity is doing the same thing day after day, but expecting different results." Benjamin Franklin, *c'est moi.*

SCENE 14

(The same afternoon, MIZINGA *and* LINDA *inside the Sainte Famille Catholic church.)*

LINDA: It's beautiful.

MIZINGA: Simple, yes. But there is a grace to it.

LINDA: Really. Just lovely.

MIZINGA: Sainte Famille is the finest church in Kigali. This is where my family and I worship. Are you Catholic?

LINDA: Me? No. I'm not much of a—

MIZINGA: I understand. You are American. Here, we are men and women of God. Catholic, Protestant, even Muslim. A few. For me, this building is our hope.

LINDA: For what?

MIZINGA: That God is still watching us. Little Rwanda, clinging to the belly of Uganda. But still, that we are not forgotten. You do not write things down?

LINDA: Oh, I don't work like that.

MIZINGA: Then how are you able to remember?

LINDA: Well, I'm not a reporter, so I don't . . . It's really not that interesting.

MIZINGA: But I am interested.

LINDA: I don't want to take up your time / talking about . . .

MIZINGA: My time is yours. I insist. Please.

LINDA: I wait for the ping. *(Off his look.)* For something that lodges in me that I can't forget. That's my starting point. My husband's work is about the mega; I'm all about the mini. We're always arguing over which is the best way to— Do you follow / what I'm . . . ?

MIZINGA: With even more interest.

LINDA: It has to be a single event. But something complex, with a multitude of meanings, that I can peel back, layer after layer, in order to—

MIZINGA: Show what is true.

LINDA: Yes! To bore down to the center of one incident until I find it: the bridge that connects something strange and impenetrable to *me*. To the world at large. Showing how connected we are / to each other.

MIZINGA: We are all the same, then?

LINDA: Well. I mean . . . on a fundamental level, / don't you . . . ?

MIZINGA: You are a bold and forthright seeker of truth!

LINDA: . . . Okay.

MIZINGA: I thank you for this. I wish to help you find your moment. To show that here, we are men and women, just like you. That this government, we, too, are dedicated to peace. Of course, there are people here who disagree with that.

LINDA: You mean with "peace" in general?

MIZINGA: Very many. It is difficult to exist with these people—angry, dangerous—but that is democracy, yes? We are following in the footsteps of our friends in the West. Belgium, France. And, of course, the U.S. We all wish to be friends with the U.S.

(GEOFFREY *enters, speaking loudly and pointing outside.)*

GEOFFREY: Did you know that street's named after Kadafi? You know, like, *Kadafi*? I mean / that's kinda—

LINDA: Geoffrey, could you please lower your voice while / we're in the . . .

GEOFFREY: Don't tell me what to do!

LINDA: I'm sorry. I was just— / Geoffrey, I'm only saying . . .

GEOFFREY: You're not in charge of me! I'm not your kid! / Dad forget to mention that when he . . .

LINDA: Well, maybe if you stopped acting like one, I wouldn't feel the need to . . . !

(They both stop abruptly. Silence. No one moves. Then . . .)

MIZINGA *(cheerily)*: Did you enjoy your goat?

(Lying simultaneously.)

LINDA: / Very interesting.

GEOFFREY: Definitely. Yeah.

MIZINGA: Next you must try the fried tilapias. *(Picking back up with* LINDA.*)* What is heartening is the progress we have made. That we can breathe easier, now that Kigali is finally a weapons-free zone.

LINDA: And the UN is enforcing this?

MIZINGA: May I speak plainly?

LINDA: Please.

MIZINGA: The UN . . . it is made up of good people, well-meaning people, but strangers who do not understand what is happening here. You read in your newspapers we are one people, we have had a civil war. But tell me, if the Russians invaded America, would you say, "Oh, this is a civil war"? No, because they are foreigners, just like these rebels. Thirty-five years ago they raped and killed us, so we forced them from this land. For thirty-five years they have lived in Uganda. They do not even speak French. These are not *Rwandais.*

LINDA: You mean the RPF?

MIZINGA: Of course. And yet somehow they are the victims. This is what the UN, their UNAMIR soldiers here, this is what they think. Please tell me, how do foreigners who invade my country, kill my people, and occupy my land, how are these to be victims? Have you perhaps heard your ping yet?

LINDA *(she smiles)*: Maybe.

GEOFFREY: What were the soldiers singing?

MIZINGA: Soldiers?

GEOFFREY: The ones we saw marching in the street.

MIZINGA: Ah! *(In Kinyarwanda.)* Turi guhiga amashu. *(Then translating.)* "We are looking" or "hunting" . . . I am not sure . . . "for cabbages."

LINDA: "We are hunting for cabbages"?

MIZINGA: Do your soldiers not chant something like this in America?

LINDA: Not lately, no.

MIZINGA: You see, this is the problem. I am translating from Kinyarwanda to French to English. So much is lost.

GEOFFREY: So if it's weapons-free and all, what's with the tanks?

MIZINGA: An excellent question. He who wishes for peace prepares for war. For us to rely on the good word of killers, terrorists armed to the teeth, who would do such a thing? *(To* GEOFFREY.*)* Would you?

LINDA: Of course not.

MIZINGA: We are still shackled to our history here. A spiral of violence. I envy you. In America, you seem to have escaped your history, and you live wonderfully well. This is my hope for my country.

GEOFFREY: Forgetting the past?

MIZINGA *(smiles)*: To wipe the slate clean and start again. *(To* GEOFFREY.*)* Come. We shall have a beer.

SCENE 15

(Later that afternoon, LINDA *at a market. She is trying out rudimentary French on a* MARKET WOMAN *selling cabbages. Standing near them is a* MARKET MAN.*)*

LINDA *(pointing)*: Excusez-moi, je voudrais acheter un chou. *(Excuse me, I would like to buy a cabbage from you.)*

(The MARKET WOMAN *smiles, picks up a cabbage, and extends it toward* LINDA.*)*

LINDA: C'est combien un chou? *(How much for a cabbage?)*

(The MARKET WOMAN *smiles, nods, and extends the cabbage again.)*

LINDA: S'il vous plaît . . . *(Please . . .)*

MARKET MAN: She does not speak French, miss.

LINDA: Oh.

MARKET MAN: She is from the country.

LINDA *(to her)*: I'm sorry. *(To him.)* Thank you. Could you ask her if—

MARKET MAN: Go, White Sox! Yes!

LINDA: Oh. You— Yes! The Sox. How do you—

MARKET MAN: I was in your country, studying. Many years ago. Chicago.

(The MARKET WOMAN *is watching them intently.)*

LINDA: Chicago!

MARKET MAN: Yes!

LINDA: I live in—my family—all of us here—we live in Illinois!

MARKET MAN: Illinois!

(He turns to the MARKET WOMAN *and speaks rapidly and excitedly in Kinyarwanda.)*

MARKET MAN: Uyu mugore lelo, n'uwo muli Amerika, hamwe nari ndi, muli Illinois! *(This woman is from America, she is from Illinois!)*

(The MARKET WOMAN *nods and smiles at* LINDA.*)*

MARKET WOMAN: Illinu!

MARKET MAN: This is what I tell my children.

MARKET WOMAN: Illinu!

MARKET MAN: That this world is wonderfully small.

MARKET WOMAN: Illinu!

MARKET MAN: Eyes open! I tell them.

MARKET WOMAN: Illinu!

MARKET MAN: In this country, if your eyes and heart are open, you will learn many things.

MARKET WOMAN: Illinu! Yis!

(The MARKET WOMAN *gestures to* LINDA *and then to her cabbages.)*

LINDA: I agree. I've found that here. Your country is so fascinating.

MARKET MAN *(translating to the* MARKET WOMAN*)*: Avuze ko igihugu cyacu ari kiza. *(She says our country is fascinating.) (To* LINDA.*)* You are kind.

LINDA: It's so beautiful here.

MARKET MAN: I am grateful to you.

LINDA: Please. It's an honor to be here. Thank *you*.

MARKET WOMAN *(to* LINDA*)*: Amashu yange nimabisi cyane. Ngaya, reba, nayasoromye mugitondo. *(My cabbages are very fresh. Here, look, I picked them from the earth this morning.)*

LINDA *(to* MARKET MAN*)*: Would you mind asking her how much for a cabbage?

MARKET MAN: Oh, no, miss. *(Pointing offstage.)* Your shopping should be done there.

(The MARKET WOMAN *is smiling and gesturing more intensely now.)*

LINDA: Why not from her?

MARKET MAN *(very politely)*: She is a filthy Tutsi whore, miss. Her cabbages will be spoiled. She will poison you, and you will die.

(Silence. The MARKET MAN *and* WOMAN *look at* LINDA.*)*

MARKET MAN *(pointing)*: There, miss.

LINDA *(pause)*: Thank you.

*(*LINDA *turns and walks off. The* MARKET MAN *and* WOMAN *watch her go. The* MARKET MAN *turns to the* WOMAN *and smiles.)*

MARKET MAN: Illinois.

SCENE 16

(Later that afternoon as well. GÉRARD *is alone in the living room of the Exley house, reading a book. He holds the text close to his face, reading slowly and out loud. His voice is quiet, and we can't make out the words.* GEOFFREY *comes into the room from inside the house. He sees* GÉRARD, *who quickly puts down the book.)*

GÉRARD: Excusez-moi, Monsieur Geoffrey. *(Excuse me, Mr. Geoffrey.)*

(As GÉRARD *starts to exit,* GEOFFREY *sees the book.)*

GEOFFREY: Whoa whoa whoa whoa whoa whoa whoa.

(GÉRARD *stops.*)

GEOFFREY: Tu lisais ce livre? *(You were reading this book?)*

GÉRARD: Oui, Monsieur Geoffrey. *(Yes, Mr. Geoffrey.)*

GEOFFREY: Tu sais lire l'anglais? *(You can read English?)*

GÉRARD: Un peu, Monsieur Geoffrey. *(I can read some, yes, Mr. Geoffrey.)*

GEOFFREY: Est-ce que tu le parles? *(Can you speak English?)*

GÉRARD: Un peu, Monsieur Geoffrey. *(Some, yes, Mr. Geoffrey.)*

GEOFFREY: So you can understand / what I'm saying right now?

GÉRARD: Forgive me. I did not mean to soil your book. I will never touch / it again. Please do not . . .

GEOFFREY: No, no, no! I didn't mean to— I'm not angry. Really. I'm not. I'm just . . . Why didn't you just, you know . . . tell us?

GÉRARD: A man who tells all is naked. A naked man is weak.

GEOFFREY: I'm down with that.

GÉRARD: . . . I do not understand / what you are . . .

GEOFFREY: Yes. I see your point. I respect that.

GÉRARD: I am sorry. My English is very poor. / My school was very short. I was not able, because . . .

GEOFFREY: No. It's good. It's . . . Sure. I understand. Yeah. You're good. Really.

(They stare at each other.)

GÉRARD *(gesturing to the book)*: May I respectfully ask what is this book?

GEOFFREY: American history. Textbook. It's called independent study. So I can graduate.

GÉRARD: You are in school?

GEOFFREY: Yeah.

GÉRARD: You are a schoolboy?

GEOFFREY: Well. I'm a senior.

GÉRARD: Here you teach yourself?

GEOFFREY: Sort of.

GÉRARD: Then you are a smart man. A smart man is a good thing.

GEOFFREY: My father says that.

GÉRARD: A father knows. Always.

*(*GÉRARD *starts to leave the room.)*

GEOFFREY: Listen. *(*GÉRARD *stops.* GEOFFREY *retrieves the history book and gives it to him.)* Keep it. Read it. Really. I've got plenty of time. I've got nothing else to do. I'm glad that we . . . I mean, it would be great if we could . . . you know . . . talk.

GÉRARD *(pause)*: You wish to talk to me?

GEOFFREY: Yeah.

GÉRARD: . . . Now?

GEOFFREY: Yes.

GÉRARD: I understand.

(Silence. No one moves. Then, off GEOFFREY*'s puzzled look . . .)*

GÉRARD: I am respectfully waiting for you to talk to me, / Mr. Geoffrey.

GEOFFREY: No! That's not what I meant.

GÉRARD: Forgive me, Monsieur / Geoffrey.

GEOFFREY: Listen. Gérard. You don't have to call me Monsieur Geoffrey. Really. I mean it. / Don't . . .

GÉRARD: Of course, sir. / I understand.

GEOFFREY: No! Not "monsieur," not "sir"—my dad is a "sir." I'm just— *(Points back and forth between them.)* We're just . . . the same. Right? I'm asking as a favor. I'd appreciate it. Okay?

GÉRARD: You are being honest with me?

GEOFFREY: Yes. I am.

GÉRARD *(he nods and smiles)*: I will read this book. I will learn of your country.

GEOFFREY: Great.

GÉRARD: Perhaps I may show you my country, if you wish.

GEOFFREY: Yes! That would be awesome!

GÉRARD: Good! / This is good!

GEOFFREY: I would love that! Totally!

GÉRARD: But if I may ask you a favor, Monsieur / Geoffrey . . .

GEOFFREY: Dude!

GÉRARD *(smiling)*: Sorry! / Sorry!

GEOFFREY *(gesturing back and forth between them, exaggerated)*: Geoff-rey! . . . Gérard! . . . / Geoff-rey!

GÉRARD *(laughing, doing the same gestures)*: Yes! Geoff-rey! Yes! *(Then:)* Please tell no one.

GEOFFREY: . . . What do you mean?

GÉRARD: My English. That I speak. That I know. I ask this as my favor.

GEOFFREY: I'm not really—I mean, / what's the big . . .

GÉRARD: The rebels speak English, all of them. If a man like me is speaking English, this man is now a suspect. It is dangerous to be confused with those people. I wish only to go about my business and bother no one. So that I may sleep at night in peace. Please. I ask this of you.

(They stare at each other. Neither moves.)

GÉRARD: Geoffrey.

SCENE 17

(Late that night, the living room of the Exley house. The sound of a phone ringing. JACK *rushes in from another room, followed by* LINDA, *and picks it up.)*

JACK *(into the phone)*: Allô, bonsoir? . . . Chuck! Hi. Yeah. I've been out looking for him all day. *(In response.)* Everywhere. What have you . . . *(Listening. Then:)* No, that's— *(Listens again.)* When? . . . How can that . . . *(Listens.)* Okay . . . Okay . . . Thanks. *(He hangs up. To* LINDA.*)* Woolsey says Joseph's clinic is closed.

LINDA: What?

JACK: Completely shut down.

LINDA: When did this happen?

JACK: He thinks a week ago.

LINDA: What for?

JACK: He doesn't know.

LINDA: Does he know where Joseph is?

JACK: He says no one does.

LINDA: Did you know that something like this / might happen?

JACK: Of course not! Do you think I would have / brought us here if . . .

LINDA: So why didn't he—

JACK: I don't know!

*(*JACK *paces.)*

LINDA: I'm sure there's a reason for all of this. Your friend will come by tomorrow, he'll explain everything. *(Pause.)* Jack?

JACK: We can't go back, Linda. The house / is rented.

LINDA: I know.

JACK: Joseph is my link. The way in. There's no book without / Joseph.

LINDA: Jack—

JACK: No book means the university is going to let me go!

LINDA: You'll find him tomorrow. / You'll go to the . . .

JACK: This isn't Sweden! *(Pause.)* Sorry.

LINDA: Listen. We're here. We've got people looking out for us. Mizinga's been very helpful. We're getting settled in. We've got plenty of food. I've even tried goat. *(Off his look.)* Oh, yeah. Side of the road, grilled, on a stick.

JACK: What did it—

LINDA: Remember that time in Cuzco when you ordered the cau-cau?

JACK *(screwing up his face)*: Oooooh!

LINDA: And afterward, you had to go to the—

JACK *(shuddering at the memory)*: Aaaaaah!

LINDA: That's what I'm talking about.

(They are smiling at each other.)

JACK: How are you so calm?

LINDA: I'm from Detroit. You think this is a big deal?

JACK: Are you going to write about this?

LINDA *(sassy, flirting with him)*: Oh, baby. You have no idea.

JACK *(flirting back)*: You gonna make me look good?

LINDA: Well, it all depends on what I get in return.

(They kiss.)

JACK *(quietly . . .)*: He's my friend, Linda. What if he's been . . .

LINDA: Listen. We're going to be okay.

JACK: How do you know that?

LINDA: Because I've got you. Whatever happens here, you've got me, and I've got you. That, I know.

JACK: I love you. So much.

(They kiss more passionately. We hear a loud car horn outside.)

LINDA: It's Geoffrey. It's just Geoffrey.

JACK: What?

LINDA: He went out. He took the car.

(The sound of the front gates being opened.)

JACK: You let him out alone / this time of night?

LINDA: He walked out the door before I knew it. / I was calling after him.

JACK: You said you would keep an eye on him. / We have to be careful here!

(The sound of a car pulling up to the house.)

LINDA: I tried, Jack. I am trying, / every day.

JACK: He's just a boy!

LINDA: He is seventeen years old! What exactly did you expect me to do? Tackle him? / Pin him down?

JACK: He doesn't know what he wants, Linda! / He's confused. We have to . . .

LINDA: You've barely seen him in three years! What do you know about / what he wants?

JACK: For God's sake!

(The sound of a car door slamming. Their volume drops instantly.)

JACK: We're his parents now, Linda! / We can't just . . .

LINDA: I am not his mother! You left her for me. Look at what he has been through. / You want to set the rules, set them!

JACK *(gesturing "stop talking")*: Shut up!

(GEOFFREY enters.)

JACK *(normal voice)*: Hey, sport.

(Silence.)

GEOFFREY: Hey.

(No one moves. Finally . . .)

JACK: So tomorrow, if either of you see Gérard, would you ask him to please tell the guard to stay in front of the house all the time / and not behind the . . .

GEOFFREY: He doesn't speak English, / Dad.

JACK: Right. Sorry. Forgot.

(Silence. No one moves.)

JACK: Do anything interesting?

GEOFFREY: Yeah.

(Silence. Again, no one moves.)

LINDA: I'm going to go in and get ready / for bed.

GEOFFREY *(gesturing off)*: That guard guy's there every night?

JACK: Yes. Just to be safe. Everyone's got one. I mean, it's not just us / because we're . . .

GEOFFREY: What's his name?

JACK: I don't know.

GEOFFREY: But he's guarding the house, right?

JACK: We'll find out tomorrow.

GEOFFREY: Did you see your friend today, the doctor guy?

JACK: We're going to meet soon. There's a lot to discuss.

(The phone rings. LINDA *quickly picks it up.)*

LINDA: Allô? *(Pause.)* . . . Allô? *(Pause.)* . . . Bonsoir?

(She hangs up the phone.)

JACK: Who was it?

*(*LINDA *gestures that she doesn't know.)*

JACK *(Pause. Then to* GEOFFREY:*)* Everything's fine.

SCENE 18

(The next afternoon, the living room of the Exley house. GEOFFREY *is teaching* GÉRARD *to sing the hip-hop song "Whoomp! [There It Is].")*

GÉRARD: "There's a party over here, a party over there . . ."

GEOFFREY: "Wave your hands in the air . . ."

(They are both doing so.)

GÉRARD: "Shake the posterior . . ."

GEOFFREY *(correcting him)*: Derriere!

GÉRARD: Derriere! *(Back into the song.)* "These three words mean you're getting busy. Who, there she is!"

GEOFFREY: No, no! "Whoomp! There it is!"

GÉRARD: Ah! *(Imitating his gestures and gusto.)* "Whoomp! There it is!"

GEOFFREY: Yeah!

GEOFFREY and GÉRARD *(together)*: "Whoomp! There it is! Whoomp! There it is! Whoomp! There it is!"

GÉRARD: I prefer Michael Jackson.

GEOFFREY: No, no, no!

GÉRARD: Michael Jackson is *fantastique.*

GEOFFREY: Dude, that's so eighties! / That's like death!

GÉRARD: He has the dances, he has the money, he has the Billy Jean. This is my dream. To be in your country with an American wife, family. Do you miss them?

GEOFFREY: What?

GÉRARD: Your family in America.

GEOFFREY: My family's all here. Me and my father.

GÉRARD: And the black wife.

GEOFFREY: Yeah, and the . . . what you said.

GÉRARD: The white wife, she is in America?

GEOFFREY: No. She's dead.

GÉRARD: This was your mother?

GEOFFREY: Yeah.

GÉRARD: I am sorry. This was—

GEOFFREY: October.

GÉRARD: May I ask how?

GEOFFREY: We were in the car. After my soccer—football—practice. We got hit by a . . . Both of us had our seat belts on. She always . . . I cut my head. That's it. Her head was . . . *(Holds out his hands in front of him.)* Have you ever seen anything like that? When someone's head just . . . *(He closes his hands together.)*

GÉRARD: Yes. My family, too. They were killed in October.

GEOFFREY: . . . Your whole family?

GÉRARD: In Burundi.

GEOFFREY: That's the country next door, right?

GÉRARD: Here we say, if you wish to know the future, look to Burundi. In October, the Tutsi there, they killed everyone they could. Until the rivers were full of bodies.

GEOFFREY: They killed . . . the Hutus?

GÉRARD: Yes.

GEOFFREY: And you're Hutu?

GÉRARD: I am pure Hutu.

GEOFFREY: Why . . . why did they do that?

GÉRARD: The Tutsi have always killed us. Stolen from us. They are cunning. Even now they are plotting behind our backs.

GEOFFREY: But why?

GÉRARD: They are afraid of us. That one day we will stand up and defend ourselves.

GEOFFREY: Could that happen here?

GÉRARD: In Rwanda?

GEOFFREY: Yeah.

GÉRARD: That is not a question for me.

SCENE 19

*(*BUISSON*'s office at the French embassy, the same afternoon. He is being interviewed by* LINDA*. A* SERVANT *enters with a tea set on a tray.)*

BUISSON: The Khmer Noir, we call these rebels. Scorching the earth, emptying the parts of the country they capture of its people. Their general, this Kagame, he is mythic here—larger than life. *(Waving the* SERVANT *off.)* Bien, bien. Ça suffit. *(Good, good. You can go.)*

(The SERVANT *leaves the tea and exits as* BUISSON *picks back up with* LINDA*.)*

BUISSON: So, what do they call him? The Black *Napoleon*!

LINDA: Well. Isn't that nice.

BUISSON: I fear, perhaps, you miss my point.

LINDA: I fear I do.

BUISSON: He is not named "the Black Ike" or "the Black Schwarzkopf"—

LINDA: Which sounds like a cocktail.

BUISSON: *Bravo, madame*—he is named for a Frenchman. Because Rwanda is part of *la Francophonie*. This is our sphere of influence. Now, of course, you wish to have influence here and to supplant us.

LINDA: Forgive me, but nobody in America even knows where Rwanda is. Do you know how much work it took to find a guidebook in English? Trust me: We don't care / about places we can't find.

BUISSON: Ah, yes. "America does not care." Indochina: You did not care. Kuwait: You did not care. Until one day, all of a sudden: How deeply you care.

LINDA: Jean-Claude, again, what I'm interested in—

BUISSON: If you are so lacking in caring, may I ask why did your government train this Kagame? Why did you teach him how to fight / so that this English-speaking soldier with his English-speaking army could invade an ally of France that has never—

LINDA: Jean-Claude . . . Jean-Claude . . . *(Cutting him off.)* Jean-Claude! . . . *(She smiles.)* I thank you for meeting with me, and for the lecture, but I'm interested in *you*. Living here, what *you* think.

BUISSON: Ah, yes. Narratives of self: Nietzsche, Montaigne, Linda.

LINDA: Time will tell.

BUISSON: Samuel said you were interesting.

LINDA: One tries.

BUISSON: Well. If I am forced to tell the truth, then I would say, living here, I have learned that freedom is vastly overrated.

LINDA: How pretty that sounds, as you like to say, but would you / be more specific.

BUISSON: These people, what is the expression? "Sold a bill of goods"? They have been convinced that above all, one must have freedom. "Freedom!" with a capital F and an exclamation point and no other thought behind it. That it is better for a people to incompetently, disastrously govern themselves than to be ruled by someone else who was at least passable.

LINDA: And you were "passable"?

BUISSON: Forgive me, but you do not even know the history of this region, and you are passing judgment. France was never here. This was a Belgian colony.

LINDA: So what do you think of them?

BUISSON: The Belgians?

LINDA: Yes.

BUISSON: Do you know how to save a Belgian from drowning?

LINDA: No.

BUISSON: Good. We had nothing to do with this nonsense. This *hypothèse Hamitique*. Measuring skulls. Handing out identity cards. You are one race, you are another race. Disastrous.

LINDA: So as the colonial power, you think the Belgians are responsible / for the problems here?

BUISSON: Ah, yes! *Le colon!* Everything is always the fault of *le colon*! Please. This is the argument of college students. This part of the world—Rwanda, Burundi, Zaire—for over thirty years the Belgians have been gone. We have been gone. For thirty years these people have made us look like saints. Thirty years they have ruled themselves, and still we are to blame? It is very convenient to blame the past. It leaves no time to deal with the present. And this, here, is a present that should be dealt with. How do you find my honesty?

LINDA: Racist and full of bullshit.

BUISSON: And I like you, too. I admire your tenacity. Your husband, it appears he is like this as well. Knocking on doors. Asking questions. Tell me, have you found this man?

LINDA: . . . No. He's still missing.

BUISSON: How unfortunate. Your husband, he must be very upset.

LINDA: That's a nice way of putting it.

BUISSON: May I continue to be honest?

LINDA: I didn't realize you'd stopped.

BUISSON: This is not America. Perhaps he would be more effective—

LINDA: If he kept his mouth shut?

BUISSON: Please. I am only offering advice, to be discarded if you wish. Discretion. One is more successful here when one is less direct. Here, the straight road is rarely the one to walk. This is not the time or the place to be a cow in the china shop.

LINDA: Bull in the china shop.

BUISSON: Even worse. If you have concerns, problems, it would be best if you came to me. The UN, your embassy, they are visitors. Strangers here. *La Francophonie.* If a thing is to be known, I will know it.

SCENE 20

(JOSEPH *appears.*)

JOSEPH: If I am honest, Jack, sometimes I wish I were just a doctor. A little practice, treating tourists with dollars and deutsche marks. That would be nice. I will not lie to you.

But who else is doing what we are doing? We are saving lives, the lives of our children. The future of this country. We are fighting to change this country, Jack. Two steps back but three steps forward. I would do anything for that. Who would not?

SCENE 21

(A bar, that night. JACK *sits with* VERBEEK, *thirty, South African. They have beers in hand and have already had more than a few.)*

VERBEEK: Compared to Sudan or Ethiopia? This used to be the East African success story. Tons of foreign aid, aid workers—

JACK: But this was before 'eighty-nine, right? When the bottom fell out of / the . . .

VERBEEK: The world coffee market—very good. Now this country doesn't have two nickels to rub together. You throw in over three years of warfare, highest birthrate in Africa, land overfarmed to the point of being useless, and now those motherfucking cocksuckers at the World Bank—you don't work for them, do you?

JACK: No.

VERBEEK: They're threatening to cut off all aid unless Habyarimana implements the BBTG in the next couple of weeks. Well, let's be honest: unless his wife and her cronies tell him to implement. And who came up with this? Because they need more tension here?

JACK: But the government's agreed to implement next week, so the peace accords are still / on track.

VERBEEK: *Agreed* to implement.

JACK: Yes, I know, but—

VERBEEK: You know how many times they've agreed to implement, then come up with a reason not to?

JACK: You're focusing on the wrong thing. The point is they've actually achieved multiparty elections here. This country has a chance!

VERBEEK: Right. And I'm Desmond fucking Tutu.

JACK: Come on! You can't be cynical about a democracy when it's just getting started. So they're being dragged to the altar kicking and screaming—fine! It's messy, but it's progress. Democratic elections!

VERBEEK: Stop talking about the fucking elections! Stop thinking like an American. This is Africa, not Delaware but with a lot of black people, all right?

JACK: I'm not from Delaware, I'm just—

VERBEEK: You think you stuff ballots in a box—presto!—problems here get solved? *(*VERBEEK *leans in closer to* JACK *and lowers his voice.)* People are being killed here *because* of the fucking elections. The UN forced them down the government's throat, they lost, now they're panicked. Now you've got Hutu elites arming private militias and hoarding weapons. They're not thinking about power sharing, they're thinking, "How many Tutsis do I have to kill to keep what's mine." The engine here's not democracy, my friend, it's violence and fear. Am I making my point, Jim?

JACK: Jack.

VERBEEK: Thanks for the beer.

JACK: You're welcome. Thanks for the *(meaning their conversation)*—

VERBEEK: You're welcome.

(They both drink.)

JACK: So how long have you been here?

VERBEEK: Just a few months. I need the UN around for my kind of work, so I don't get shot at. Collecting information on human rights abuses doesn't make you particularly popular.

JACK: Where were you before this?

VERBEEK: Mogadishu.

JACK: That must have been—

VERBEEK: Yeah.

JACK: So . . . why do you keep doing it?

VERBEEK: Same reason you're here.

JACK: What do you mean?

VERBEEK: Well, what are *you* running away from?

JACK: Nothing. I wanted to come here.

VERBEEK: Right. Because Paris was full, and you thought, "Hmmm, where else do they speak French? Rwanda! That's good." You alone?

JACK: No, I brought my family.

VERBEEK: You get more interesting by the beer. So what do you teach?

JACK: Poli-sci.

VERBEEK: You got tenure?

JACK: You know about the tenure / system?

VERBEEK: I been around, yeah.

JACK: I'm tenure-track.

VERBEEK: Your age, you're still track?

JACK: My son was born when I was in grad school, so I took some time off to— It's not that / uncommon.

VERBEEK: You coming up for review?

JACK: After I'm back.

VERBEEK: First time?

JACK: Second, / actually.

VERBEEK: Aaaaah.

JACK: That's why I'm here. Research for that book. That I need to finish. Well, start and finish.

VERBEEK: So you're on sabbatical.

JACK: . . . Unpaid leave, / actually.

VERBEEK: You just get better and better.

JACK: There wasn't enough time to submit a proposal. I had to call in favors just to get my courses covered.

VERBEEK: So it's publish or perish.

JACK: Exactly.

VERBEEK: Sort of like a blade to your throat.

JACK: Thank you, yes. When you don't get tenured the first time, you beat on doors just to *get* a second position. Someplace you used to think you wouldn't be caught dead teaching at. So you move. You uproot your entire life. And your wife is less than pleased, because the sacrifices to *her* career—and God bless her that she would, but now there's this, this, this *thing* between you, because you've changed the rules, this wasn't the plan. And the clock is ticking, and then—out of the blue!—there's three of you under the same roof now. So you have to bring him here, too! And you have no idea how to even *talk* to him, because his mother, the wife you fucking left, has been—and the clock is ticking—and you—AAAAAAAH!

(Silence.)

VERBEEK: So everything's riding on this book. About the guy.

JACK: Yeah.

VERBEEK: Who's not here.

JACK: He's *here*. He's just—

VERBEEK: Not here.

JACK *(pause)*: Yeah.

SCENE 22

*(*JOSEPH *appears.)*

JOSEPH: What is hardest, my friend, is the struggle to be patient. In the face of . . . so much. I am *Rwandais*, Jack. No people in the world are as patient as we are. But even I have my limits. I know you are not a praying man, but I find myself doing that more often now. God and medicine: How dearly one needs them both in this life.

SCENE 23

(Late that night, the living room of the Exley house. A ringing phone. LINDA *enters from another room and quickly picks it up. She does not see* GÉRARD *enter as well.)*

LINDA: Allô? . . . Allô? . . . Bonsoir?

(No one is there. She puts the phone down as . . .)

GÉRARD: Excusez-moi, / madame . . .

LINDA: Ah! God . . . I'm sorry, Gérard. I didn't see you there.

GÉRARD: Il y a une jeune femme qui désire vous voir tout de suite. *(There is a woman here who says she must see you.)*

LINDA: Gérard, I'm sorry, I have told you— *(Slow and loud.)* I do not speak French.

GÉRARD *(repeating himself, slow and loud)*: Il y a une jeune femme qui désire vous voir tout de suite.

(A Rwandan WOMAN *enters.)*

GÉRARD *(gesturing to her)*: Là voici. *(Here she is.)*

(No one moves as the woman stares at LINDA.*)*

LINDA: . . . Bonsoir.

WOMAN: Good evening.

LINDA: Oh! Good evening. *(Pause.)* May I help you?

WOMAN: Yes, please.

(No one moves.)

LINDA: I'm sorry, I don't think we've—

WOMAN: I am Elise Kayitesi. I am Joseph's wife.

End of Act One.

Act Two

SCENE 1

(The living room of the Exley house, later that night. ELISE *and* JACK *sit in chairs.* LINDA *stands to* JACK*'s side.)*

ELISE: That day, nothing was different. We were to go to dinner after his rounds. I had dressed and was waiting for him.

LINDA *(to* JACK*)*: This was last Monday.

ELISE: Yes, over a week ago. *(To* JACK.*)* He has spoken many times of you. Your friendship. I have sent our children to Butare to be with my family. Joseph is Tutsi, so our two sons are considered Tutsi. It is best they are not here, in case their father has been . . . I do not understand this.

JACK: I'm so sorry.

ELISE: Things have been quiet since he was freed from prison. He has had no troubles with / the government.

JACK: Joseph was— What?

LINDA: Your husband was in prison?

ELISE *(pause)*: Yes.

LINDA: When was this?

ELISE: Three years ago, when the RPF first crossed into the country from Uganda and the fighting began. Men came, Joseph was taken.

JACK: Why?

ELISE: . . . I do not know why he did not tell you this. Joseph is a good husband. A good father. / He is . . .

JACK: I know that, Elise. Of course. Do you need a place to stay? / You're welcome to.

ELISE: No, thank you. I must be at home. In case there is any word.

LINDA: Have you been to the police?

ELISE: The police are not to be spoken with now. Not for someone like me. Only someone else, someone who is not from here. Only he could find answers.

JACK: *I'll* go to the police.

LINDA: Yes. We'll / talk to the police. We'll find out something.

JACK: I'll talk to Woolsey again. / Christ, I'll go to UNAMIR!

ELISE: Thank you! Yes! I thank you so much!

*(*ELISE *rises to leave.)*

LINDA: We'll call you tomorrow.

JACK: As soon as I hear anything. I promise.

ELISE: Please. Even if you know nothing.

(No one moves for a moment. ELISE *turns to leave, then back to them.)*

ELISE: My husband is a doctor. He has helped so many people.

(She is gone.)

LINDA: How long have they been married?

JACK: I didn't even know he was married.

LINDA: What?

JACK: I don't remember him ever . . . It never came up.

LINDA: Like how being in jail never came up?

JACK: Yes. Exactly.

LINDA: Jack, how long have you known this man?

JACK: He's my friend, Linda.

LINDA: What kind of friend hides things like this? What kind of a man is that?

SCENE 2

(A police station, the next morning. JACK *is in midmeeting with a Rwandan* POLICEMAN.*)*

POLICEMAN: Gasana.

JACK: Joseph. That's what I said, Officer.

POLICEMAN: He has the AIDS sickness, this doctor?

JACK: No. No, he wants to stop the spread of— He treats people.

POLICEMAN: Tutsi. This doctor works with Tutsi.

JACK: Everyone. Anyone / who's suffering.

POLICEMAN: Hutu do not get AIDS. AIDS is a Tutsi sickness. Perhaps you did not know this.

JACK: Sergeant, my friend is—

POLICEMAN: I am a captain.

JACK: Sorry, I didn't mean to be rude.

POLICEMAN: He is your friend, this Tutsi?

JACK: Yes.

POLICEMAN: I see. *(He writes something down.)* And you have tried to call him?

JACK: Many times.

POLICEMAN: You have been to his office / and to his house?

JACK: Yes. Yes. Dr. Gasana has not been seen in over a week. Something has happened. I am reporting him missing.

POLICEMAN: He has gone to Uganda.

JACK: What? How / do you . . .

POLICEMAN: They all go to Uganda. This is where the *ibyitso* are. Where they are coming from. All of these Tutsi doctors, they are *Inkoytanyi*. Milk drinkers. Killers. And now these foreigners, they have made our president, that spineless Habyarimana, grovel and give them our land. They are killing my beautiful, beautiful country. You and your UN and your Bill Clinton, you do not know this. Why does Bill Clinton not know this? We are busy. We do not have the manpower for this. We are preparing to cleanse this country. You are better off without this man. Trust me.

SCENE 3

(The Mille Collines, that afternoon. JACK *and* WOOLSEY *poolside.)*

WOOLSEY: What did you offer him?

JACK: What do you mean?

WOOLSEY: The cop, how many francs. *(Off* JACK*'s look.)* What, they don't have bribes in Sweden?

JACK: Dammit. I didn't even think to— / Christ. Like a tourist.

WOOLSEY: It's okay, it's all right. No harm, no foul.

(A WAITER *has entered with two glasses and two bottles of beer. As* WOOLSEY *and* JACK *speak, the* WAITER *opens the beers and pours them.)*

WOOLSEY: Okay. So you've been to all the hospitals, you've talked to his wife, you've asked around: no word.

JACK: He wrote that he'd be free after the first weekend. That he'd meet me on Monday at the hospital. He was going to arrange for a cook, a driver, a translator for my—

WOOLSEY *(to the* WAITER*)*: Merci.

WAITER *(in Kinyarwanda)*: Umunsi umwe uzanywa inzoga nkabagabo. Inzoga Primus! *(One day you will drink Primus, like a real man!)*

*(*WOOLSEY *and the* WAITER *laugh as the* WAITER *exits.)*

JACK *(gesturing toward the* WAITER*)*: What did he just say?

WOOLSEY: No idea.

JACK: But you just—

WOOLSEY: Jack, the only Kinyarwanda I know is *yégo*, *oya*, and *byeri*: "yes," "no," "beer." *(Off* JACK*'s look.)* Because it doesn't matter. You're working on a book, I'm working on a pension. We're just a presence here. On a map, this country's so small, "Rwanda" has to be written outside the borders. Little arrow pointing to it, saying "Actual country, don't forget!" When did you last hear from him?

JACK: A week ago. This letter, confirming everything. He was my college roommate.

WOOLSEY: Interesting.

JACK: What is?

WOOLSEY: A Tutsi doctor, speaks English, college in the States, not France or Belgium: pretty uncommon. Almost odd, don't you think?

JACK: I guess.

WOOLSEY: When's the last time you saw him?

JACK: In person? Decade, maybe. We fell out of touch three years ago. Nothing. Then two months ago, out of the blue, he contacted me.

WOOLSEY: Fell out of touch?

JACK: Yeah.

WOOLSEY: Any idea why?

JACK *(pause)*: No. He must have just . . . No.

WOOLSEY: Jack, things are different here. People, even people we think we know . . . they're not the same here as when they're away from here.

JACK: You're saying—

WOOLSEY: You may not have the whole picture.

JACK: Meaning?

WOOLSEY: You don't have the whole picture. A lot can happen to someone in ten years. You need to face facts: He's a prominent Tutsi, doing work that made him stand out. The tall nails are the ones getting hammered here, Jack. You should prepare for the worst.

SCENE 4

*(*LINDA *and* ELISE*, at a table inside the Mille Collines, later that afternoon. A* WAITER *is opening a bottle of wine and pouring two glasses as they speak.)*

LINDA: I'm sorry.

ELISE: Please.

LINDA: We'll know something about Joseph soon. I'm sure of it. Jack is— *(To the* WAITER*.)* Merci.

ELISE *(to the* WAITER*)*: Murakoze. *(Thank you.)*

LINDA: I have a contact at the French embassy myself. / I wanted to tell you this in person. And for us to have a chance to just talk. For you to have a moment away from everything.

ELISE: I am grateful for your help. It has been a blessing. Thank you. Yes. Of course. Yes.

(The WAITER *leaves as* LINDA *picks up her glass of wine, gesturing to* ELISE *to do the same. She does.* ELISE *holds back as* LINDA *takes a sip.)*

LINDA: Oh my God!

ELISE: Yes.

LINDA: This is the worst—

ELISE: Yes. I did not want to be rude. Certain things do not translate here. *(Gesturing to the wine.)* This would be one.

LINDA: May I ask you a question?

ELISE: Of course.

LINDA: What's it like being married to a Tutsi? *(Off* ELISE*'s look.)* I'm sorry if that's . . . While I'm here, I'm trying to really talk to people. So I can understand this place and write something that's specific. Honest. For a Hutu like yourself, to have a Tutsi husband who's been incarcerated— My God, I can only imagine the pressure you're under. I'm asking as a woman married to a man of a different race. Trust me: I know about—

ELISE: You are blunt.

LINDA: That's a nice way of putting it.

ELISE: Like my husband. Joseph says this is a trait he acquired in America. He says he has tried to shake it off, but it is like a dog that will not let go of his leg.

LINDA: I've been accused of having more than a little pit bull in me.

ELISE: You are to write about this?

LINDA: Yes.

ELISE: All of this?

LINDA: Yes. Elise, / you can trust . . .

*(*ELISE *leans in.)*

ELISE: Joseph says we are Banyarwanda. All of us. Tutsi, Hutu, these are *fabrications politiques.* You understand / what I mean by this?

LINDA: I do, yes.

ELISE: The same religion, language. Hutu marrying Tutsi, Tutsi marrying Hutu, Twa marrying / both.

LINDA: Twa?

ELISE: Ce sont des pygmées. *(They are Pygmies.)* But there are even fewer Twa than Tutsi.

LINDA: You're saying there aren't that many Tutsi?

ELISE: Here most of us are Hutu. But if you look at us, you cannot even tell from which group we are. Before the Belgians came, Joseph says, "Tutsi" was just the word for anyone with power; "Hutu" was the word for anyone without.

LINDA: But what do you think?

ELISE: Joseph is much more articulate on this subject. *(She leans in closer, lowering her voice.)* He says that the Tutsi have been made the enemy because it is easier to have an enemy than to find a solution. That since the war started, all of the Tutsi in this country are like hostages. They are seen / as traitors simply for . . .

LINDA: I want to hear what you think, Elise.

ELISE: For who?

LINDA: I'm sorry, / I'm not . . .

ELISE: For who are you writing? It would be best if I know who I am speaking to before I choose what to say.

LINDA: Just the truth, as you see it.

ELISE *(in Kinyarwanda)*: Ukuri kwose sikwiza. *(Then translates.)* "To speak truth is good, but to speak all truth is not."

LINDA: I understand, but—

ELISE: No, you do not. If people like you understood, this country would be very different. We are beaten, we are starved, we are killed, and you do nothing. You do nothing, and so it means nothing. To you, we are nothing. *(Pause.)* Now I have become blunt, too.

LINDA: I'd say so.

ELISE: It feels quite good.

LINDA: I can see that.

ELISE: I will do this again.

LINDA: I think that's a good idea.

ELISE: If I am to be killed, I wish to save my children. If Joseph is dead, if I am dead . . . *(She hands* LINDA *a piece of paper.)* These are their names. My sons. This is where they are. In Butare. Please do not let them die.

SCENE 5

*(*GEOFFREY *and* GÉRARD *at a nightclub full of* PATRONS, *late that night. They have beers in hand and are yelling over loud, pulsing Zairian pop. A Rwandan* MAN *stands near them, drinking as well.* GÉRARD *gestures across the room at a young Rwandan* WOMAN *who is dancing.)*

GÉRARD: You like that one, yes?

GEOFFREY: Yeah, she's hot!

GÉRARD: Hot?

GEOFFREY: Totally!

GÉRARD: Hot is good?

GEOFFREY: Very good!

GÉRARD: The Tutsi women, they are all hot. The legs, the breasts. I only sex with Tutsi!

GEOFFREY: She's Tutsi?

GÉRARD: Look at her, look at me. Can you not see?

GEOFFREY *(He cannot.)*: Okay, but your family.

GÉRARD: Yes.

GEOFFREY: In Burundi.

GÉRARD: Yes.

GEOFFREY: By Tutsis.

GÉRARD: Yes.

(Before GEOFFREY *can go on,* GÉRARD *turns and gestures toward the* WOMAN.*)*

GEOFFREY: Whoa! Don't— What are you doing?

GÉRARD: You do not like her? She must be Hutu?

GEOFFREY: No! I just— Dude, I don't know enough French!

GÉRARD: Geoffrey, she is not interested in your French. You must pay her afterward.

GEOFFREY: . . . What?

GÉRARD: After you are serviced. If you have dollars, that would be best. Welcome to Rwanda, Geoffrey!

(The WOMAN *has danced her way in front of* GEOFFREY. *She smiles and reaches out.* GEOFFREY *looks at* GÉRARD, *then takes her hand. She leads him out onto the dance floor, and they begin to move together. The music heats up. She sways, flirting, touching; he tries to keep up.* GÉRARD *watches them. The Rwandan* MAN *does, too. The* WOMAN *and* GEOFFREY *yell over the music to hear each other.)*

WOMAN: Vous dansez bien pour un blanc qui vient d'arriver. *(You dance very well for a white man who has just arrived.)*

GEOFFREY: Je suis désolé. Je suis americain. Je ne parle pas— *(I'm sorry. I'm American. My French is not very—)*

(The WOMAN *throws back her head and laughs, then dances closer to* GEOFFREY, *winding her arms and legs around him.)*

WOMAN: Tu aimes ça? Et ça, tu aimes? Est-ce que tu me trouves sexy? *(Do you like this? And this? Do you find me sexy?)*

(They are pressed together skintight, as she bumps and grinds to the music and he tentatively touches her. The Rwandan MAN *grows agitated by this.* GÉRARD *tries to calm him down. We cannot hear their words. Then, suddenly, the* MAN *yells at the* WOMAN.*)*

MAN *(in Kinyarwanda)*: Vana intoki zawe kuri uwo muzungu, wa ndayawe! *(Get your arms off that white man, you whore!)*

(The WOMAN *laughs and swivels her hips at the* MAN.*)*

WOMAN *(in Kinyarwanda)*: Ufite ishyari, wa mbwawe! *(You're just jealous, you dog!)*

MAN *(in Kinyarwanda)*: Ziba wa ndaya we y'umututsi! *(Shut your mouth, you Tutsi bitch!)*

(The WOMAN *and a confused* GEOFFREY *keep dancing. The* MAN *lunges, but his way is blocked by* GÉRARD, *trying to defuse. The* MAN *yells over the music.)*

MAN *(in Kinyarwanda)*: / Nzagaruka, Nzagucamo kabiri! Urunva wa karayawe, nzagucamo kabiri! *(I'll be back to cut you! I'll cut you in two, you hear me, whore? In two!)*

GÉRARD *(in Kinyarwanda)*: Ntakibazo. Ntakibazo. Uyu musore ni umushyitsi wacu, ntampamvu yo guhangayika. *(It's okay. It's okay. The boy's a guest in our country. No reason to lose your cool. Relax.)*

(As GÉRARD *eases the apoplectic* MAN *out of the club, the* MAN *gestures toward the* WOMAN *and runs his thumb violently across his throat. The music heats up. The* WOMAN *pushes even closer to* GEOFFREY.*)*

WOMAN *(in halting English)*: Do you want to sexy me?

GEOFFREY: Yes.

WOMAN: Do you condom?

GEOFFREY: No, I . . . *(Realizing.)* Yes. Actually, I— I mean, I wasn't planning, but I—

WOMAN: Will you protect me?

GEOFFREY: Yes. I mean, sure. *(Pause.)* Yes.

(She smiles, takes him by the hand, and starts to lead him upstairs.)

SCENE 6

(UNAMIR headquarters at Amohoro Stadium, early the next afternoon. JACK *stands waiting in a hallway as a Bangladeshi* MAJOR *brushes past.)*

JACK: Excuse me. Officer! / Excuse me!

MAJOR: Sir, you must have an appointment. / I am sorry, but I am too busy to meet with—

JACK: I have been waiting outside your office for four fucking hours!

MAJOR: Please do not curse, sir! There is no need for cursing. *(Pause.)* I am sorry to hear about this. This is a worrisome thing. My condolences to you, Mr. Exley.

JACK: Thank you.

MAJOR: Now you must go to the police and fill out / the paperwork for . . .

JACK: I have been to the police!

MAJOR: Then you must go again, that is how things are done in this—

JACK: First he doesn't exist. Then he vanishes. Then he's supposed to have gone off to Uganda to, to, to drink milk and start killing people because—I don't know! This man is my friend. Something has happened to my friend. You are the UN, and I am an American citizen! I have come for help! So help me!

(They stare at each other.)

MAJOR: Please take off your jacket.

JACK: My . . . ?

MAJOR: Take . . . off . . . your . . . jacket. *(Pause. Then* JACK *does so.)* Lift your arms. *(He does.)* Turn around. *(He does.)* Thank you. You may sit. *(Jack does so.)* One must be careful here about taping and such things. Now, shall we be honest?

JACK: Please.

MAJOR: Mr. Exley, do you speak French?

JACK: No.

MAJOR: If you will forgive me, that is very foolish. You are seeking answers in a country you do not know, without a language to understand it. And yet you wish me to send my soldiers, who have just arrived from Bangladesh. You would like us to run through this city, flashing guns, saying, "A man is missing, and an American wants to know!" "An American! Oh my goodness. Shaky, shaky, shaky: Here he is." Mr. Exley, we are a small, dirty Band-Aid on a large, festering wound. I am sorry to be so explicit, but I want to be very clear. You promise me you are not taping this?

JACK: Yes. I promise.

MAJOR: What do you think we can do here?

JACK: Help? Protect?

MAJOR: Oh my goodness. We are instruments, Mr. Exley. My soldiers, my superiors. For an instrument to be used, there must be a will to do so. For there to be a will, the world must care. This country, these people, do you think the world cares?

JACK: I do. Absolutely.

MAJOR: I see. The American soldiers killed last year in Somalia. You know about this?

JACK: Of course.

MAJOR: Eighteen men, slaughtered. Terrible. But did you know about the ninety UN soldiers killed trying to save those Americans?

JACK: . . . No, I didn't.

MAJOR: Pakistani and Malaysian soldiers. They were killed, and their penises were cut off and put in their mouths. Do you know what a terrible death this is for a Muslim, Mr. Exley? Do you not find it interesting that you have not even heard of this? These were not "marauding savages," terrorist-something-or-others. They were soldiers. Ninety UN soldiers. Unfortunately, with my complexion, Mr. Exley. If their deaths did not matter, what help is there for your friend? He is missing, he has been killed—the world does not care. This is a terrible truth, but it *is* true. A black African man. In this world, what is that? Something not even seen by the eyes of God. I am sorry your friend is Rwandan. I am sorry you are here to know that. I am sorry for this entire rotten business. Good luck to you.

(The MAJOR *turns to leave.)*

JACK: Officer.

MAJOR *(turning back)*: Yes?

JACK: What's your name?

MAJOR: How would you know my name? You have never met me.

SCENE 7

*(*LINDA *and* MIZINGA *on the street, the same afternoon, sightseeing Kigali.)*

MIZINGA: Do you smell that?

(He gestures for her to join him in taking a deep breath. They breathe in and out together.)

MIZINGA: After it has rained like this, what do you smell?

LINDA: It's . . . uh . . .

(He gestures for her to take another deep breath; she does so.)

LINDA *(exhaling)*: Earth, and / a, a, a sort of charcoal, and a, a, a—

MIZINGA: . . . Yes . . . Good . . . And . . . ?

LINDA: Eucalyptus!

MIZINGA: That is it! You see? You are becoming *Rwandaise*! This is the smell of my country. If I am to show you everything, you must know this, too. I hope you will write all of this. For your country to know my country. I would give my life for this land, Linda. A man must hold his country here, in his heart. He must give his sweat and his blood so that . . . *(Off* LINDA*'s look.)* Have I said some / thing amusing?

LINDA: No! What you're saying is moving. I only wish I could . . . It's just, where I live, people like me don't have your level of conviction. Even talk like that makes us / embarrassed.

MIZINGA: I understand. The world is different for you. We are not so lucky. We have a saying here: In Kigali, life expectancy is twelve hours, renewable.

LINDA: We have a saying like that back home *(being "ghetto")*: Yo, watch your back.

MIZINGA: . . . Yo, wash / your . . . ?

LINDA: No, no, no. *(Hitting the words intently, with full hand gestures.)* Yo! Watch your back!

MIZINGA *(imitating her)*: Yo! Watch your back! *(Considers it.)* I like this. I will use this. Now you are the teacher. I thank you / for this.

LINDA: Thank *you*, Samuel. *(Gestures around her.)* For all of this. Being here—God! This is exactly what I needed. I mean, look at me! I look like you. For once I'm not "the other." My husband, for once he's the . . . Ooooohkay. Way too much / information.

MIZINGA: Please. We are friends now, Linda. Friends tell each other everything.

LINDA: It's just, all the pressure we've been under, with Jack having to write this—and now, with Geoffrey! I'm not equipped for this stepmother business. I'm trying. I just don't know how to . . .

(She stares at him. Neither moves.)

LINDA: You listen with such intensity, Samuel.

MIZINGA *(staring back at her)*: We are all listeners here, Linda.

LINDA: I'm not used to that.

MIZINGA: To you? How could a man not listen.

LINDA: I'm in love with this place, but I'm also scared of it. Can I admit that to you?

MIZINGA: I believe you just did.

LINDA: The dichotomy here is . . . vertiginous. Such beauty, such unbelievable . . . But then things I've heard. Seen. I'm trying to reconcile. I feel a part of this place now, Samuel. I want to understand this place. But I can't / seem to . . .

MIZINGA: All of life is here, Linda, in one small place. Everything that is said, everything that is done in this world, is in Rwanda. That is why life is vivid here. And fearsome. The air is sweet because of this; we are grateful for the time God gives us. You do not understand this place because, where you live, you are too fortunate. You lack an adversary.

LINDA: You're saying . . . I need an enemy?

MIZINGA: One is defined by what one is against. And who. To struggle against these people, to fight for what is yours. To suffer and yet to struggle on: This is what makes life precious. And brings understanding. *(He offers her his hand.)* Come. I wish to show you something.

SCENE 8

*(*JACK *and* VERBEEK *again at the bar, later that afternoon. The men are in midconversation, beer glasses in hand.)*

JACK: Who saw this? Who told you this?

(A WAITER *enters and comes toward them with a fresh bottle of whiskey.)*

VERBEEK: Some UNAMIR boys. Wanted to pass on what they'd seen. One of the villages they went through, they found . . .

*(*VERBEEK *stops as the* WAITER *arrives, ceremoniously undoes the cap, then sets down the bottle between them.* VERBEEK *waits until he leaves, then jumps right back in.)*

VERBEEK: . . . about two dozen people killed.

JACK: Tutsis?

VERBEEK: That's what they were told. They said the men were cut up with machetes or had their heads cracked open with *masues*, these clubs with nails that— You get the picture. The women had their Achilles tendons cut. So between rapings, they couldn't run. Some of the women who were killed were pregnant. Their stomachs were cut open.

JACK: Jesus. Who did it?

VERBEEK: Don't know. Hutu Power militias, government troops—but something is happening.

JACK: Who are you going to tell?

VERBEEK: I'm telling you, aren't I?

JACK: But you have to put this in a report. People have / got to know about this.

VERBEEK: This isn't enough for a report.

JACK: What are you talking about?

VERBEEK: First rule of reports: You get various sources, and you get them confirmed. That's how you find a pattern. That's the only way your narrative makes sense.

JACK: But you're not writing a fucking novel. / You can't just bury this.

VERBEEK: You want me to write this without proof?

JACK: You can't pretend / you didn't . . .

VERBEEK: Did I see it? Did you see it? Do you know it happened?

JACK: These are UN observers, / for Christ's sake! Why would they lie?

VERBEEK: Yes, yes, yes. *(Off "lie.")* Because everyone lies here. I'm lying to you right now.

JACK: About what!?!

VERBEEK: I'll let you know when I remember. *(He pours them each a drink.)* Everyone lies here, Jack. You'll start, too, if you haven't already, Mr. I'm Not Running Away from Anything. It's self-protection. The question while you're here is: Why would this person be honest? Why would he risk that? *(Pointing to the bottle in front of them.)* You see how they always bring a fresh one, unscrew it in front of you?

JACK: Yeah.

VERBEEK: Now we're supposed to take our first sip together. It's tradition. So we know there's nothing extra in there.

JACK: . . . Poison? Are you serious?

VERBEEK: You mean am I lying to you? *(He gestures to their glasses.)* Let's find out.

(They lift their glasses. A moment, then JACK *drinks first. As they put their glasses down . . .)*

VERBEEK: Someone saw your friend.

(JACK *stares at him.)*

JACK: Who saw him?

VERBEEK: I asked around, and someone said that someone saw him. That's all I'll say.

JACK: Recently?

VERBEEK: Yes.

JACK: I mean within the last week?

VERBEEK: Yes.

JACK: Okay. Good. Okay. *(Off* VERBEEK*'s look.)* What?

VERBEEK: People didn't want to talk about him. His name made them frightened.

JACK: Frightened? He's a doctor. He runs a pediatric AIDS clinic.

VERBEEK: They linked him to serious business, Jack. Passing on information about weapons caches.

JACK: To who? Who is he / supposed to be . . .

VERBEEK: I'm just telling you what I heard.

JACK: Jesus! The man is missing, and no one can give me a straight answer! Woolsey says he's probably dead; you tell me this; Mizinga / tells my wife that . . .

VERBEEK: *Samuel* Mizinga? You're kidding, right?

JACK: No. What's the problem?

VERBEEK: Samuel Mizinga is CDR.

JACK: I don't know / what that means. I don't speak French.

VERBEEK: *Coalition pour la Défense de la République.* They're the Hutu extremist party. They wouldn't even sign the Accords. Jack, Samuel Mizinga makes Idi Amin look like a choirboy. He's one of the people calling for the streets to be washed in Tutsi blood.

JACK: How do I know this is true?

VERBEEK: Well, now you're getting a handle on things.

SCENE 9

*(*LINDA *on the street with* MIZINGA, *even later that afternoon. They stare out past us at a large building. We hear the sounds of soldiers and military equipment.)*

LINDA: Are those soldiers actually RPF / guerrillas?

MIZINGA: Yes.

LINDA: And they've taken over your parliament / building?

MIZINGA: The soul of our nation, yes. Like a rebel army in your White House. Can you imagine? A battalion of killers, with guns and missiles.

LINDA: My God, how horrifying. How could this—

*(*LINDA *has started to move forward, but* MIZINGA *puts his arm out, stopping her.)*

MIZINGA: Please. Do not cross this line. Everything on that side has been seized by the RPF. There you are no longer safe. They are digging tunnels underneath the earth, Linda, preparing for an attack. Reinforcements, ammunitions, smuggled in every night / under darkness.

LINDA: Samuel, I / don't . . .

MIZINGA: It is important you see this. To understand. This is why we are frightened. That what has just happened in Burundi will happen here: Hutu, everywhere, murdered in the streets, the earth soaked in their blood. This Tutsi army. They have been attacking us, trying to overthrow, for so long. To push the Hutu back down, so again we are nothing but slaves. These terrorists, who Habyarimana—that peasant—has allowed to infect this city, who are protected by your UN, they are everywhere.

Neighbors, so-called friends. Even in families, loving families, there are *ibyitso*. *(Pause.)* Joseph Gasana.

LINDA: . . . Do you . . . How do you—

MIZINGA: A killer of Hutu children.

*(*LINDA *stares at him.)*

MIZINGA: Why do you think his clinic was closed? Giving medicine only to Tutsi, so that our children would die. You have been deceived. I am sorry for that. I know this must be difficult, but you must trust me. You do not know this country.

SCENE 10

(The police station, that evening. JACK *sits before the same* POLICEMAN, *who puts on a big show of looking through the papers in front of him.)*

POLICEMAN *(reading from a report)*: Gasana, Joseph.

JACK: Yes.

(The POLICEMAN *continues to read silently.)*

JACK: Captain, you called me. I came out this time of night / because . . .

POLICEMAN: Ah, the Tutsi doctor.

JACK: Yes! What have you heard about him?

POLICEMAN: Yes. We know now, yes.

(They stare at each other as we also see a room above the nightclub. The WOMAN *who was with* GEOFFREY *the night before leads him into the room by the hand.)*

JACK: Where is he?

POLICEMAN: Here.

WOMAN: J'ai envie de toi. *(I really like you.) (Pointing to a chair.)* Assieds-toi. *(Sit down.)*

(GEOFFREY *sits as* JACK *pulls out his wallet, takes out francs, and hands them to the* POLICEMAN.*)*

(The POLICEMAN *counts the francs as the* WOMAN *stands behind* GEOFFREY *and begins to massage his shoulders.)*

(The POLICEMAN *starts to exit to the back of the police station. As* JACK *starts to follow . . .)*

POLICEMAN: Wait.

(The POLICEMAN *exits as the* WOMAN *pulls* GEOFFREY*'s shirt off over his head and drops it on the floor.)*

WOMAN: T'es vraiment costaud. T'es un vrai mec. *(You are very strong. You are like a real man.)*

(The POLICEMAN *returns with a gurney bearing a body covered in a white sheet. The part of the cloth covering the face is red with blood.* JACK *stares at the body.)*

(The WOMAN *begins to massage* GEOFFREY*'s bare chest as the* POLICEMAN *lifts the cloth.* JACK *looks down on the figure. The sheet is put back down.)*

WOMAN: Tu veux essayer autre chose? *(Would you like to try something different?)*

(GEOFFREY *nods, and the* WOMAN *crosses and kneels in front of him, her back to us. She undoes his pants and begins servicing* GEOFFREY *as the* POLICEMAN *shows* JACK *what looks like a small passport.)*

POLICEMAN: His identity card was in his trouser. Down around his ankles. He was found on the side of the road, where these men go to see their Tutsi whores.

(The POLICEMAN *wheels the body off as the* WOMAN *stops for a moment.)*

WOMAN: Est-ce que tu aimes ça? *(Do you like this?)*

(GEOFFREY *nods, and she goes back to it as the* POLICEMAN *returns.)*

POLICEMAN: What can we do? These cockroaches: They breed with each other, then kill each other. It is their blood, this sickness.

(The WOMAN *continues, and* GEOFFREY *is breathing heavily.)*

JACK: I want an investigation into his murder.

POLICEMAN: Sir, I am telling you, there is nothing to be done.

JACK: I will go to my embassy, do you understand? Do you understand?

(The WOMAN *is moving faster now.* GEOFFREY*'s breath is hard, sharp.)*

POLICEMAN: Kigali is a very dangerous city. I am sorry to be the one to tell you this, Mr. Jack William Exley living in Nyamirambo, on sector Nyakabanda, in the house with the blue door. Terrible things can happen here.

*(*GEOFFREY *spasms, throws his head back, and gasps.)*

SCENE 11

(Late that night, JACK *and* WOOLSEY, *at* WOOLSEY*'s house.)*

WOOLSEY: Who else have you talked to about this?

JACK: No one. I came here, from seeing the . . . Jesus.

WOOLSEY: I'm sorry, Jack. Truly sorry. So. Your book. What are you gonna do?

JACK: Fuck my book! The man is dead. His face wasn't even . . .

WOOLSEY: You go home. Tell Linda and your boy to stay put. I'll speak to UNAMIR, see if they can spare a couple of men, just to check in with you the next few nights. Everything's going to be fine.

JACK: "Fine"?

WOOLSEY: For your family. Look, I understand / that this has been a hell of . . .

JACK: I want this investigated. I want to find who—

WOOLSEY: We're not going to do that. *(The two men stare at each other.)* This isn't our country. We don't make the rules here. You're going to have to let this go. A man was in the wrong place at the wrong time. Tragic. Truly.

SCENE 12

(The living room of the Exley house, very late the same night. In the dark, we can make out the form of a MAN*, sitting in a chair. After a moment,* JACK *enters from outside. He closes the front door. As he starts to cross the room . . .)*

MAN: Hello, / Jack.

JACK: Jesus!

MAN: I hope you are well.

(The men stare at each other. Neither moves.)

JACK: Joseph?

JOSEPH: You look like you have seen a ghost. I am not a ghost.

*(*JACK *crosses to a lamp to turn it on.)*

JOSEPH: Please.

(A moment, then JACK *takes his hand off the lamp.)*

JACK: I thought you were dead.

JOSEPH: Yes.

JACK: You're not dead.

JOSEPH: Forgive me, but you say this like it is not a good thing.

JACK: How long have you . . . Did you plan this?

JOSEPH: Jack, this is me. / Joseph.

JACK: Where have you been? / Why didn't you call me?

JOSEPH: It is only me, I am nothing but me. *(Off "call me.")* I have tried to call you. Many times. But it was never you who answered. I have been waiting for a moment to see you. When it was safe for me.

JACK: Now that you're "dead."

JOSEPH: Yes.

JACK: Who was that I saw?

JOSEPH: I do not know. I have prayed for him.

JACK: So you faked . . . What is this?

JOSEPH: I am just trying to stay alive.

JACK: Because people—

JOSEPH: Yes.

JACK: Why?

JOSEPH: I have lists. Of names. People who are to be killed. Hundreds of people. Help me, Jack. Please.

JACK: Do you know these people?

JOSEPH: Of course. Everyone knows everyone in this city.

JACK: So who are they?

JOSEPH: They are like me: doctors, lawyers, teachers. Some are Hutu, some are Tutsi.

JACK: So none of them are affiliated with—

JOSEPH: Yes, some are politicians. / But they are moderates, they are the people who are trying to . . .

JACK: I mean are any of them involved in any kind of secret / political . . .

JOSEPH: "Secret"? Yes, Jack. We are all secret agents. My code name is Chuck Norris.

JACK: So what have they done?

JOSEPH: Nothing. That is the problem. We are in a civil war, Jack. To not choose a side, this is as bad as choosing the wrong one.

JACK: So who's behind these lists? The government? The Interahamwe? CDR's militia?

JOSEPH: Very good, my friend. For me they are all the same. They are all Hutu Power: extremists and extremist-extremists. They are arms of the same octopus.

JACK: So who am I supposed to trust?

JOSEPH: Besides me, you mean? You are like me, Jack. We are outsiders. Teacher, doctor. You are not French, Belgian, NGO. You have no history here. That is a gift. A weapon.

JACK: Joseph. What am I supposed / to do?

JOSEPH: You are American. You will be listened to.

JACK: For God's sake! I'm / just an academic!

JOSEPH: Jack! You can get these lists into the hands of people who will protect. You can get my family and me out of this country. Only you.

(They stare at each other.)

JACK: Okay. Okay, so I'll go to the UN. I've / been there, already met a—

JOSEPH: No, they are useless. Paper soldiers.

JACK: UNAMIR's got two thousand armed—

JOSEPH: MINUAR, Jack. The French acronym is MINUAR.

JACK: They've got soldiers / who can—

JOSEPH: In Kinyarwanda, it means: "Your lips are moving, but you are saying nothing." It is good to know that someone in the UN has a sense of humor.

JACK: Then I'll go straight to the French embassy and / meet with . . .

JOSEPH: Jack! Please! Open your eyes. You have not been paying attention.

JACK: They're the only ones with connections! There are fifteen

U.S. officials in this entire city. The French can / find out whoever's behind this.

JOSEPH: Their soldiers fought the RPF! There is only still a war because of the French! Mitterrand's own son is selling the weapons that are killing our women / and children!

JACK: WELL, WHAT THE FUCK, JOSEPH! WHAT THE FUCK!

(The two men check that no one has been woken by JACK*'s outburst. Silence. The coast is clear. They hug.)*

JOSEPH: It is so good to see you. I am sorry, my friend. There was no one here I could turn to. Who else could I / trust with . . .

JACK: My son is here, Joseph. My wife and / my son.

JOSEPH: I told you to come alone, Jack. If I had known, I would never have—

(The sounds of a car honking and the front gates being opened.)

JACK: It's okay, it's okay! Joseph! It's just Geoffrey. / He goes out and—

JOSEPH: Jack, no one can know I'm alive.

JACK: Of course. / This way.

JOSEPH: Not even Linda.

JACK: Joseph, I have to. She's my wife.

JOSEPH: She has been talking to the people trying to kill me, Jack.

JACK: What?

JOSEPH: They know everything she says and does. Trust me!

(Before they can exit into the house, GEOFFREY *enters from outside and stops when he sees the two men. No one moves.)*

GEOFFREY *(to* JOSEPH*, in Kinyarwanda)*: Mwiriwe. *(Good evening.)*

JOSEPH: Good evening.

GEOFFREY: Oh. Cool.

(No one moves.)

JACK: Geoffrey, / this is—

JOSEPH *(to* GEOFFREY, *in Spanish)*: ¿Puede ser que hablas español, joven? *(Do you speak Spanish, perhaps, young man?)*

GEOFFREY: Uh . . . *(In Spanish.)* Un poco. Sí. ¿Cómo lo sabes? *(Some. Yes. How did you guess that?)*

*(*JOSEPH *points at* GEOFFREY*'s Che Guevara T-shirt.)*

JOSEPH: Tu camiseta. ¿Admiras al Che? *(Your shirt. Do you admire Che?)*

GEOFFREY: Fue un regalo. De esta chica. *(It was a present. This girl.)*

JOSEPH: ¡Ah! Un regalo de una chica. ¿Era bonita? *(Ah! A present from a girl. Was she pretty?)*

GEOFFREY: Sí, era bonita. *(Yeah, she was pretty.)*

JOSEPH: Un regalo de una chica bonita. Eres dos veces bendecido. *(A present from a pretty girl. You are twice blessed.)*

GEOFFREY: ¿Usted es el médico? *(You're the doctor?)*

JOSEPH: I am one, yes.

GEOFFREY: That Dad's writing his book on?

JOSEPH *(pause)*: I am he.

GEOFFREY: How's it going?

JOSEPH: Splendidly.

(No one moves. Finally . . .)

JOSEPH: I must be going. *(To* GEOFFREY.*)* It was very nice to meet you.

JACK: Go in the back, Joseph.

*(*JOSEPH *and* JACK *stare at each other.)*

JOSEPH *(to* JACK*)*: Thank you, my friend. *(He turns and looks at* GEOFFREY. *Pause. Then in Spanish:)* Un placer. *(A pleasure.)*

(JOSEPH *exits into the house.*)

JACK: Geoffrey. I need to / ask you—

GEOFFREY: What's going on?

JACK: Everything's fine. I promise. I don't want you to tell anyone you've seen that man.

GEOFFREY: Not even Linda?

JACK: No one. I need you to trust me. I need to be your father right now. Please give me your word.

(Neither of them moves.)

GEOFFREY: Okay.

SCENE 13

(GEOFFREY *and* GÉRARD *in the car, the next morning.* GEOFFREY *is driving.*)

GÉRARD: Slowly! Slowly! / These dirt roads, you will crack the chassis! You should not go driving when you are angry, Geoffrey.

GEOFFREY: Sorry. Forgot. Sorry. Look, I'll be more careful!

GÉRARD: A woman should not speak to you like that.

GEOFFREY: Don't worry about it.

GÉRARD: Stand in your way, try to block you from going out. Jumping about like some chicken.

GEOFFREY: I said it's cool!

GÉRARD: Cool?

GEOFFREY: Yeah.

GÉRARD: Cool . . . ?

GEOFFREY: Means good.

GÉRARD: Like hot?

GEOFFREY: Exactly.

GÉRARD: Cool is good *and* hot is good?

GEOFFREY: Yes.

GÉRARD: *Fantastique!* When I go to America, I will say *(pointing)*, "This is cool" and "That is hot," and I will sex all the women. *(Off* GEOFFREY*'s laugh.)* Why not?

GEOFFREY: All of them?

GÉRARD: Yes!

GEOFFREY: Dude, we got a lot of women!

GÉRARD: You watch me, Geoffrey! I will sex the black woman, the white woman, the thin woman, the fat woman—mmmm! The fat American woman! *(Making thrusting sounds and hip movements.)* Mmmm! Mmmm! *(Off* GEOFFREY*'s laughter.)* Ah, ah, ah! This is your problem.

GEOFFREY: What? / What are you talking about?

GÉRARD: You are embarrassed. Look at you: You are a pink man now. I see you. I watch you. You talk about a woman like you talk about a man. Treat a woman like a man. Like there is no difference. Did God not make us different? You give away your power, Geoffrey!

GEOFFREY: Dude, I'm not / giving away anything.

GÉRARD: Then why did you let the black wife speak to you like that?

GEOFFREY: Look, she's my / dad's wife.

GÉRARD: You should not let the black wife—

GEOFFREY: Linda. Her name's Linda. And don't— She's not black. She's African-American.

GÉRARD: . . . I do not understand.

GEOFFREY: We don't say "black" anymore. We say "African-American."

GÉRARD: She is from Africa?

GEOFFREY: No. Her people—you know, at one time her ancestors were— It's just what we say, to be respectful.

GÉRARD: Of who?

GEOFFREY: Of . . . the people . . . who . . . I don't know.

GÉRARD: But she is American.

GEOFFREY: Yes!

GÉRARD: She is not African, she is American. You are American, I am African. How can one be African and American? If you are American, you are American. Who does not know this?

GEOFFREY: Yeah, but she's an American *and* she's— Okay. In America, okay, the white people, you know, like me, we have the power. We control . . . pretty much everything. So—

GÉRARD: Ah! You are Tutsi! The white man is the Tutsi! / *(Joking.)* I am in the car with a Tutsi!

GEOFFREY: No, man! That's not what I'm—

GÉRARD *(putting his head out the window, pretending to cry for help)*: Aaaaaah! Tutsi! Aaaaaah! *(Back to* GEOFFREY.*)* You are like the man hiding in your house.

*(*GEOFFREY *stares straight ahead.)*

GEOFFREY: What are you talking about?

GÉRARD: The Tutsi your father is hiding. Who is he hiding from? Why would he need to be hiding?

GEOFFREY: How did you know he's—

GÉRARD: I am frightened, Geoffrey, to be in your house with this man. I am too frightened to sleep in your house. Here, no one is sleeping in their houses. In our village at night, my wife is taking our children to the church.

GEOFFREY: You have a . . . what? Why aren't they / —I don't . . .

GÉRARD: Home is not safe. Everyone is waiting.

GEOFFREY: For what?

GÉRARD: I pray to know. But God does not tell me. You are my friend.

GEOFFREY: I know.

GÉRARD: I am your friend.

GEOFFREY: Yeah. Totally. *(Looks at him.)* Yes! Of course.

GÉRARD: Then I am asking you.

GEOFFREY: What do you mean?

GÉRARD: To go. To leave with you. I will get my family, and we will—

GEOFFREY: Gérard, I'm not—we're not going anywhere. / We just got here. My dad's book isn't even . . .

GÉRARD: You will leave soon, Geoffrey. Do you think this is a place for you to stay? Something is coming! Closer, closer. I do not wish to be here to see it. I will do what I must. But to go, I would only need—

GEOFFREY: You want me to, to take you to—

GÉRARD: Please.

GEOFFREY: I'm just . . . What can I do? I'm just a . . . I mean . . . What can I do?

(They drive in silence as they stare straight ahead.)

GÉRARD: I understand.

SCENE 14

(The driving range at the Kigali Country Club, later the same morning. WOOLSEY *is dressed to play, club in hand.* JACK *has just arrived, out of breath.)*

WOOLSEY: Jack! What, are you stalking me now?

JACK: I called your office. / They said . . .

WOOLSEY *(getting ready to hit a ball)*: Christ, I wish you played. I always get teamed up with some Belgian. Ever played competitive sports with a Belgian? There's a reason the whole empire thing never worked out for those people. And the French! The way they treat the caddies is . . .

(He unwinds and hits his ball. The two men watch the long, arcing shot go on and on. Then WOOLSEY *drops another ball and continues.)*

WOOLSEY: . . . unbelievable. Like they think they're still running this part of the world. That little Parisian snot Jean-Claude, out here / last week . . .

JACK: I have some information.

WOOLSEY: Since last night?

JACK: Yes.

WOOLSEY: Something you want to tell me?

JACK: Yes.

WOOLSEY: Good. Okay. *(Pause.)* Is this a twenty-questions thing? Because / I can—

JACK: People are going to be killed. There are lists.

WOOLSEY: . . . Of people?

JACK: I've seen them, yes, hundreds of people. These are Hutus and Tutsis. All walks of life. They're not involved in— Regular people. Something is going to happen.

WOOLSEY: I know.

(They stare at each other.)

JACK: / You—

WOOLSEY: I live here, Jack.

JACK: So . . . ?

WOOLSEY: What?

JACK: . . . *Stop this.*

WOOLSEY: Jack, I've told you. We are strangers here. There are two hundred fifty Americans here. This whole country, that's it. / There are two hundred fifty million of us back home. Whatever is going to happen here, how important do you think—

JACK: I am coming to you. I am a citizen. I am reporting a crime to you. Men and women are going to be killed. I am a citizen, and *(cutting him off)* you are my fucking government!

(They stare at each other.)

JACK: So help me, I will find a way to—

WOOLSEY: Go over my head? Call in the marines? Okay.

(WOOLSEY goes back to his game and drops another ball. He rears back, club over his shoulder, ready to hit—then turns to JACK.)

WOOLSEY: You gonna send your son with them?

JACK: What?

WOOLSEY: These lists. What would you give up to save these people, Jack? Would you send Geoffrey?

JACK: That is not—

WOOLSEY: Ho, ho, bullshit, yes, it is. Boots on the ground, mission of mercy, we sweep in—who's the "we," Jack? Some trying-to-make-it-to-college kid from the Bronx? Some eighteen-year-old cow-tipper from Illinois? They should come here? Risk their lives to save some people on some list because it's the right thing to do? You teach poli-sci, Jack. When, in the history of the world, has there been a country with a foreign policy based on "It's the right thing to do"? People are killed. Every day. All over the world. That *is* the world, Jack. Would that it were not. Who gave you these lists?

(They stare at each other.)

JACK: I don't know them.

WOOLSEY: Someone who knew your doctor? The one who's supposed to be dead?

JACK: I never saw them again.

(Neither man moves.)

WOOLSEY: When you find yourself in a hole, Jack, stop digging. I made some phone calls this morning. I have some things to tell you about your doctor friend. You're gonna want to hear them. Trust me.

SCENE 15

(The Exley home. Same day, same time. LINDA *and* ELISE, *who is shaking.* GÉRARD *stands to one side.)*

ELISE: Again, I am so sorry / to bother you. But this is where I had to come.

LINDA: Please. Please. It's fine. I just wish I knew where Jack was. I got up this morning, he was already off doing—God knows what.

ELISE: The men, I don't know how they entered. I woke up, and they were—

LINDA: Did they hurt you? Did they—

ELISE *(she shakes her head vigorously)*: No.

LINDA: Was anything stolen?

ELISE: They were not there for that. They were searching. Under the bed, the bathroom, the kitchen storeroom. One of the men had a gun. He put it in my face. "Your husband is a traitor. When I find him, he will die slowly."

LINDA *(dismissing him)*: Merci, Gérard.

(GÉRARD *exits.)*

ELISE: I must go to Butare. From there I will try to get our children to Burundi. Please tell Joseph this. Tell him they know and they are coming for him.

LINDA *(stopping her)*: Elise. Last night Jack got a call from the police. He had to identify a body. It was Joseph's.

*(*ELISE *stares at her.)*

ELISE: This is not true.

LINDA: I'm so sorry. I know this / must be . . .

ELISE: That body was not Joseph's.

LINDA: . . . How do you . . . ?

ELISE: Your husband told me this.

*(*LINDA *stares at her.)*

ELISE: He phoned me late last night to tell me Joseph was alive and somewhere safe. He warned me of the lists and promised me he would give them to the people who will protect us.

LINDA: What lists?

ELISE: Those who are marked to die. Why has your husband not told you all this?

(They stare at each other.)

ELISE: Please ask him to tell Joseph where I am going.

(She starts to leave, then turns back.)

ELISE: Do not trust a husband who does not trust you.

SCENE 16

(Sound of a thunderclap, a downpour. The living room of the Exley home, late that afternoon, dark from the storm. GEOFFREY *is crossing to the front door—then stops. He realizes someone else is in the room.)*

GEOFFREY *(in Kinyarwanda)*: Ninde uri munzu? *(Who's there?)*

*(*GEOFFREY *turns on a light, revealing* JOSEPH.*)*

JOSEPH: You have Carol's facility with language.

GEOFFREY: When did you meet—

JOSEPH: When you were a child. I held you in my hand. Your mother put you in this one hand. You were delicate and so very small. I am sorry, Geoffrey. I liked her very much. Where are you going?

GEOFFREY: Out.

JOSEPH: With your father and Linda not here? Do they know / you are . . .

GEOFFREY: Just going to see someone.

JOSEPH: The same "someone" you were seeing last night?

GEOFFREY: Why is everyone here killing each other?

JOSEPH: Rats and cats, cats and rats.

GEOFFREY: That one doesn't really translate.

JOSEPH: For the rat, there is no animal more dangerous than the cat. It is all he sees, all he thinks of. Because the cat, he spends each day trying to kill the rat. For if he does not, and the rats become more and more, who will be the hunter then? It is not hatred that drives us both, it is fear. We are trapped in a cycle. Prisoners, of each other.

GEOFFREY: Have you killed people?

JOSEPH: Of course not. I am a doctor. I am a man like your father.

GEOFFREY: I don't know my father.

JOSEPH: He is your father. What else do you need to know? Who has been here?

GEOFFREY: You mean / visiting my—

JOSEPH: Yes. To see Linda, your father.

GEOFFREY: Or me? Like who's been visiting me?

JOSEPH: Have you had visitors?

GEOFFREY: Is there a reason I should tell you that?

JOSEPH *(gesturing offstage)*: The one waiting for you in the car, who is *that* man?

GEOFFREY: Gérard works here.

JOSEPH: And you trust him?

GEOFFREY: Yeah.

JOSEPH: You are fortunate.

GEOFFREY: He's my friend.

JOSEPH: Then you are twice blessed.

GEOFFREY: What are you doing here?

JOSEPH: I am staying here.

GEOFFREY: Why?

JOSEPH: Some things one should not ask. Trust is to be earned. Is it not?

SCENE 17

*(*BUISSON*'s office, the French embassy, late the same afternoon. The sound of rain.* BUISSON *and* LINDA *are midconversation.)*

BUISSON *(reading from a folder)*: Kayitesi.

LINDA: Elise Kayitesi. I want to know if there's a way she and her children / can be protected.

BUISSON: May I ask what you know of this woman.

LINDA: She's a Hutu. She's, she's just a mother. Elise isn't affiliated with any sort of— She's not involved in anything.

BUISSON: And where is she now?

LINDA: She's on her way to Butare.

(They stare at each other.)

BUISSON: Linda, I cannot help if you have so little information.

LINDA: This is her address.

*(*LINDA *hands him* ELISE*'s piece of paper.)*

BUISSON: And the husband?

LINDA: He's dead.

BUISSON: What did he do? His business here?

LINDA: I don't know anything about him. Just that he's dead.

BUISSON: Who have you spoken to about this?

LINDA: I'm speaking to you.

*(*BUISSON *puts down the folder.)*

BUISSON: I will make phone calls. / I will inquire and see what can be done . . .

LINDA: Thank you. Thank you so much.

BUISSON: . . . if you are honest with me. This was the doctor. This "dead" husband. Yes? The one *your* husband—

LINDA: I've never met him. Please believe me. I don't know / anything about this man.

BUISSON: "Man is evil, but woman is base."

LINDA: . . . Excuse me?

BUISSON: Our friend Friedrich / Nietzsche.

LINDA: Yes. Right.

BUISSON: I do not agree, of course, but I admire his honesty. And now I am going to continue down *our* path of honesty. These people here kill each other, Linda. Violence is always beneath the surface. Like a watch, ticking. Those in power kill those out of power with an almost biological regularity. They are tribal. It is in the blood. This is shocking and brutish, yes, but it is also true. It is my job to protect people like you and help those on our side.

LINDA: "Our side"?

BUISSON: Do not confuse diplomacy with missionary work, Linda. In this world, sides are always chosen.

LINDA: She's a woman with two children.

BUISSON: Whose husband you know nothing about. You have no context, Linda, and as we discussed, that is a dangerous thing. Joseph Gasana is a spy for the RPF. He is a terrorist, with blood on his hands.

(He takes out another folder from his desk.)

BUISSON: Things that have not been seen, they are hard to imagine. I think you should see these things. Perhaps then you will wish to tell me everything you know, to help us find this man.

(He slides the folder across to her.)

BUISSON: Understand, Linda: You are now involved with serious business. As serious as it gets.

SCENE 18

(That night, GEOFFREY *and the* WOMAN *in the room above the nightclub. The sound of rain mixes with throbbing music from downstairs. They have had sex and are getting dressed. The* WOMAN *is on her knees;* GEOFFREY *is standing and has been drinking.)*

GEOFFREY: My dad took me. Him and my mom. When I was a kid. This island. Waaaaaaay out. These beaches, and it was so still, you know? Can't forget something like that. The, the, the clarity! Can you understand what / I'm saying?

WOMAN: I sexy good?

GEOFFREY: Yeah, Emiritha, I've got more francs.

(He takes out his wallet and gives her money. He stares at her.)

GEOFFREY: I thought this was gonna . . . *(Gestures between them.)* This was gonna be about you and / . . . It's not like that. You know? It's all just . . .

WOMAN: Tu vas me protèger, Geoffrey? *(Will you protect me, Geoffrey?)* Tu m'amènes / avec toi? *(Will you take me / with you?)*

(The music downstairs has stopped, and we hear people chanting in the distance.)

GEOFFREY: Yeah, yeah, yeah. Just let me finish my—

WOMAN: Tu les entends? / Ils approchent! *(Do you hear them? / They are coming!)*

GEOFFREY: Listen! Okay? I'm just, I'm just trying to—what are we, people like me, supposed to— / You know what I mean? This fucking country is just . . . sorry . . . I don't understand why everyone here is . . . I don't want to be here.

WOMAN: S'il te plait, Geoffrey, il faut que j'aille avec toi! *(Please, Geoffrey, I must go with you now!)*

(Kneeling in front of him, she frantically begins to undo his pants.)

GEOFFREY: I don't understand this place. I hate this fucking place!

(GEOFFREY shoves her away and exits, leaving her in the room.)

SCENE 19

(JACK and VERBEEK, the same night, moments later. They are again at the bar, midscene. We hear the rain coming down fiercely outside.)

JACK: Joseph Gasana. What exactly have you heard?

VERBEEK: I told you what I could. People said he was mixed up with dangerous things.

JACK: I've just been told things about Joseph. Specific things I need to corroborate / to know if . . .

VERBEEK: Look! I'm sorry that your friend is dead, but—

JACK: He's not.

VERBEEK: . . . Okay.

JACK: So, please: Who told you, and what exactly / did they . . .

VERBEEK: Jack! Maybe your friend's who you think he is, maybe not. Maybe he's done things, maybe not. You want to be certain? You let him take the first drink.

(As VERBEEK *starts to leave,* JACK *grabs his arm.)*

JACK: I need your help. I have lists of people. / I have no one else I can—listen to me!—names of people in this city who are going to be killed!

VERBEEK: No. I can't do that. That would compromise my position. I don't— Stop telling me. Stop— *(Off "names," silencing him.)* Shut up. Shut up! You want to get involved, that's your choice. You think you can make a difference, go ahead. I don't get involved. Because I have seen what happens.

SCENE 20

(The room above the nightclub, moments later. The WOMAN *is waiting for* GEOFFREY *to come back.* GÉRARD *and the* MAN *from the club enter the room. The* MAN *has a machete.* GÉRARD *covers the* WOMAN*'s mouth and helps the* MAN *drag her out of the room, downstairs, and through the empty nightclub.* GÉRARD *watches from the doorway as the* MAN *takes the* WOMAN *out the front door and offstage.)*

*(*GÉRARD *watches the* WOMAN *be killed. He turns back into the nightclub.)*

GÉRARD: Geoffrey . . . Geoffrey!

(GEOFFREY *enters from upstairs.)*

GEOFFREY: Hey! Where's the music?

GÉRARD: I should not have brought you here. I am sorry.

GEOFFREY: Where is everybody? / What happened to all the . . . ? *(He mimes people dancing.)*

GÉRARD: Geoffrey, we must go now.

GEOFFREY *(pointing toward the front door)*: Where's Emiritha? / Is she already . . . ?

GÉRARD: She is gone. *(Pointing toward the back door.)* We go this way now.

*(*GEOFFREY *goes toward the front door.)*

GEOFFREY: No, I didn't pay her enough. Can't be rude like that.

*(*GÉRARD *puts himself in* GEOFFREY*'s way, trying to stop him.)*

GEOFFREY: / Gave her the wrong color bill— *(Shoving* GÉRARD.*)* Get the fuck off me!

GÉRARD: Come—Geoffrey—Geoffrey—

*(*GEOFFREY *pushes past him and goes to the front door. He sees the* WOMAN*'s body.)*

(Neither man moves. GEOFFREY *puts his hands over his mouth.)*

GEOFFREY: She . . . she's . . .

GÉRARD: God is not watching us now, Geoffrey. We are alone. We all must do what we must do.

SCENE 21

(The living room of the Exley house, very late that night. JACK *and* LINDA *are midargument.)*

JACK: You did what?

LINDA: Jack, I gave her my word! / I can't just sit here and do nothing while everything is—

JACK: Mother of God, Linda! What were you thinking?

LINDA: What? Exactly what, Jack? What did I do wrong?

JACK: The French are not to be trusted. / Not here. We can't . . .

LINDA: "The French"? You're making statements like "the French" now? This is all the rage in political science? "The French," / "the Africans," where else can we go with this?

JACK: We have to, we have to be careful. This isn't—

LINDA: Detroit? Thank you. I was so confused about that.

JACK: You know / what I mean.

LINDA: I don't know one damn thing!

(Neither moves.)

LINDA: Where is he?

(They stare at each other.)

JACK: I don't know.

LINDA: Don't. Don't. Where is he?

*(*JOSEPH *enters from inside the house.)*

JOSEPH: Good evening. I am Joseph. You must be Linda. It is an honor to meet you.

*(*LINDA *stares at him.)*

LINDA *(to* JACK*)*: How long has he been here?

JACK: Linda, people are looking for him. What did you want me to do?

LINDA: What did I want / you to . . . ?

JOSEPH: Linda, you cannot trust the CDR. Samuel Mizinga is a killer.

LINDA *(to* JOSEPH*)*: Are you part of the RPF?

JOSEPH: I am a doctor. I work with children / who are sick from HIV.

LINDA: Children? You work with children? *(To* JACK.*)* He let Hutu babies die, Jack. So he could save all the medicine for the Tutsi / children in his clinic.

JOSEPH: That is a lie! You think we have medicine for everyone? Have you learned nothing here? I could only give treatment to those who had a chance to live. I am to save half from one group, half from another? My patients are not Hutu, they are not Tutsi, they are children!

JACK: Joseph. Answer the question.

JOSEPH: Do not forget who we are, Jack. It is me, Joseph. It is only me.

JACK: Are you involved / with the RPF?

JOSEPH: Are my hands clean? Is this what you want to know? Am I spotless? Is that what you need me to be? Hands as white as yours?

LINDA *(to* JOSEPH*)*: I have been shown photos of bodies. People killed by the RPF. / People you helped to have murdered!

JOSEPH: Those were government soldiers killed! / Not women, not children, but rapists and killers!

JACK: Jesus, Joseph!

JOSEPH: I gave information. That is all. The RPF is trying to save this country, Jack. Not Hutu, not Tutsi, but all of us. We have no choice but to fight until—

LINDA: It's "we" now? / Now it's turned into "we"?

JACK: How could you lie to me like—

JOSEPH: Open your eyes! Where do you think you are! *(To* LINDA.*)* The people who have whispered in your ear, who you tell things to. Do you know what they will do if they find my children? *(To* JACK.*)* You think I stopped writing because I was too busy? The RPF entered the north to liberate, and I was jailed for being a doctor and a Tutsi. In a hole, chained like an animal. Beaten for sport.

JACK: Why didn't you tell me?

JOSEPH: They let me out, you think I am free? People are watched. Letters are read. I wrote everything to you—*between* the lines. How could you not see?

LINDA *(to* JACK*)*: I don't trust a word out of his—

(Blackness as the lights cut out. The sound of a gunshot in the distance.)

JACK: Jesus Christ. What was, / what was—what is that?

JOSEPH: The generator. Jack, go! Turn on the generator.

(Another gunshot. The sound of a car pulling up and honking over and over.)

JOSEPH: / Quickly! You must!

LINDA: Is that Geoffrey? Jack! Is that Geoffrey?

JACK *(to* LINDA *as he exits into the house)*: I don't know!

(Sound of a car door slamming.)

(Sound of gunfire. Closer.)

GEOFFREY *(offstage, calling from outside)*: Dad! . . . / Dad! . . . Dad! There are people outside! Lights are out! Everywhere!

LINDA: We're in here, Geoffrey! We're in here!

(Sound of gunfire. Closer. Sound of GEOFFREY *rushing in.)*

LINDA: Are you / okay?

JOSEPH: What are you seeing / out there?

GEOFFREY: There's no guard! The guy, he's gone! The gates are wide open! Where is everyone? What's going on? There are men coming down the street with machetes and clubs!

JOSEPH: What is the uniform?

(Lights snap on. LINDA, JOSEPH, *and* GEOFFREY *in the room.)*

JOSEPH: Boy! What are / they wearing!

GEOFFREY: Nothing! There's no uniform! They're just—clothes—and—

(Sound of smashing glass from offstage.)

JACK *(offstage)*: Jesus!

(All turn as JACK *enters.)*

LINDA: Jack! Are you all right? / What happened?

JACK: Someone threw a rock through the— It almost hit me in the head!

JOSEPH *(to* GEOFFREY*)*: Where is your friend?

(All look at GEOFFREY.*)*

JOSEPH: Where is your friend, Geoffrey?

(Sound of gunfire. Closer.)

GEOFFREY: Gérard was with me. Isn't he here?

JOSEPH: Pick up the phone, Jack. Please, pick up the phone. You are an American citizen. Please, Jack. Now.

*(*JACK *goes to the phone, picks it up. The phone is dead. He tries to make it work.)*

JACK: Dammit dammit dammit / dammit dammit dammit dammit!

JOSEPH *(to* GEOFFREY*)*: What did you tell him? Your friend, what does he know!

(Bam. Bam.)

(A knocking on the front door.)

(Silence. No one moves.)

(Bam. Bam. Bam. Louder this time.)

(No one moves.)

(The door is kicked open. MIZINGA, *the* MAN *from the embassy party, and* GÉRARD *enter. The* MAN *holds a rifle.* MIZINGA *and* GÉRARD *hold machetes.)*

MIZINGA: Good evening.

(No one moves.)

MIZINGA: Dr. Exley. Linda.

LINDA: Samuel. Gérard.

JOSEPH *(in Kinyarwanda)*: Niko mwa bagabo mwe, ndabona twibeshye, reka mbere ke uko— *(Gentlemen, there's obviously been some sort of mistake. If you'll allow me to—)*

MAN *(at* JOSEPH *in Kinyarwanda)*: Ziba, wa cyitso we! *(Silence, Icyitso!)*

MIZINGA: I am sorry to disturb your evening. Tonight there is trouble all over Kigali. We are doing all we can to protect those who need to be protected. And our friends.

(Pause.)

LINDA: Thank you, that's / . . . thank you.

JACK: We're fine. No need. Really.

MIZINGA: The patriot Martin Bucyana has been killed.

JACK: . . . I'm sorry, we don't / know who . . .

MIZINGA: A man who kept his country here, in his heart. Whose life has now been taken by terrorists. Tonight, all over this city, there will be a reckoning. We will take what we have come for, and we will not disturb you any longer.

*(*JACK *moves to stand in front of* JOSEPH.*)*

JACK: This man is our guest.

MAN *(in Kinyarwanda)*: Uwuhe muntu? / Ntamuntu mbona. Nyenzi gusa mbona hano. Umugambanyi ufite amaraso y'uburozi. Mbwira, mugihugu cyanyu, inyenzi muzikoza icyi?

MIZINGA *(translating)*: "What man? I see no man. This is only a cockroach here. A traitor whose blood is poison. Tell me, in your country, what do *you* do with cockroaches?" I am only translating, you understand.

JACK: This is our home.

MIZINGA: Yes. It was my pleasure to find it for you.

JACK: I am asking you to leave.

MIZINGA: This is not your business. It does not concern you. *(Turning to look at* LINDA.*)* I am sorry your eyes could not be opened, Linda. I apologize for my failure.

JACK: No one is leaving.

LINDA: Jack, don't—

JACK *(to* LINDA*)*: Shut up! *(To* MIZINGA.*)* What are you going to do? Shoot us? You think you can just shoot us? Do you have any idea what would happen if—

MIZINGA: Please. Of course not. But this is a wanted man. A killer of Hutu children. I cannot be responsible for the people outside this house. What they will do if I were to leave without him. Let us not try that. No one wishes for that.

LINDA *(to* MIZINGA*)*: We have lists. Names of people. You can have them. / Just leave. Please. Take them and—

JACK: Linda! No! For God's sake! Don't say another—

LINDA *(to* JACK*)*: We do not belong here! This is not our problem!

MIZINGA: Thank you, but that is not necessary. Do not worry about the lists. We have lists of every single cockroach in this nation. And one day soon we will start hunting cabbages.

(The MAN *cocks his rifle and starts moving toward* JACK *and* JOSEPH.*)*

JOSEPH *(in Kinyarwanda)*: Nyabuna, ndabinginze! Bararengana, ntacyobakoze! *(Please! I beg you! These are innocent people! They have done nothing!)*

(At the last moment the MAN *turns and points his gun at* GEOFFREY, *who falls to his knees.* JACK *tries to lunge toward him, but* JOSEPH *steps in the way, grabbing him. The* MAN *pushes the barrel of the gun into* GEOFFREY*'s head.)*

(All overlapping:)

MAN *(in Kinyarwanda)*: / Tuzuzuz' amaliba n'amaraso yabo hanyuma tuboherez' iwabo muli Ethiopia! Ntabwo tuzongera kub'abaja! *(We will fill the rivers with bodies and send them all back to Ethiopia! We will not be slaves again!)*

JOSEPH: / Jack! They are bluffing! They would never do it! Don't let them—

JACK: / Please! Please don't! Please!

LINDA: / Oh my God oh my God oh my God oh my God.

GEOFFREY: Dad! Dad! Don't let them! Please! Don't let them— *(Over everything:)* DADDY!

*(*JACK *thrusts* JOSEPH *off him.)*

JACK *(to* MIZINGA*, pointing at* JOSEPH*)*: TAKE HIM!
TAKE HIM!
TAKE HIM!

(No one moves.)

JACK: Take him. Please.

(The MAN *slowly rotates his rifle until it is trained on* JOSEPH*.* GÉRARD*, machete in hand, crosses to* JOSEPH *and grips him.)*

*(*GEOFFREY *is still on his knees.* JACK *goes to him.* LINDA *starts to go to* JACK *and* GEOFFREY*, then stops.)*

MIZINGA: This will mean nothing to you soon. All of us, we will mean nothing. This is so unimportant to you. You will go home and forget. How fortunate you are.

(The lights dim on the room. Bodies in tableau.)

(A light on JOSEPH*, who turns and speaks to us.)*

JOSEPH: We say here, Jack, that every day God strides the earth, but at night he returns always to sleep in Rwanda. He has given us so much, it is hard sometimes to dwell on what we have done with those gifts. The past here is an argument; the future, unknown. But today, in the present . . . I have hope.

Your true friend, Joseph Gasana.

(The lights fade to darkness.)

(End of play.)

What Came After: A Postscript

"There are no stangers in Rwanda." A journalist told me this late at night in a bar in Kigali, the capital of this tiny African nation. I had gone there in February 2006 to finish preparing *The Overwhelming*.

A play for me begins with a question I don't know how or am afraid to answer. I had wanted to write a play set against the events of the Rwandan genocide for twelve years because of such a question. In the spring and summer of 1994, as I watched and read about the killings that engulfed Rwanda, I kept asking myself the following: If *you* were there right now, what would *you* do to stay alive? What kind of person would you prove to be?

Ten years later, in the summer of 2004, I began work on my play. I set my story in Kigali in early 1994, on the eve of the genocide, when all the factors that led to the killings were in place but few understood the scope of what was about to happen: eight hundred thousand mostly Tutsi citizens slaughtered by their Hutu countrymen in a hundred days. Setting it then was a necessary constraint for the scope of my play. But as I researched and wrote, I also learned about the Rwanda of the last decade. Gradually, it was what came after the genocide that began to haunt me as much as the killings themselves.

How do you move on from a nightmare of bloodshed when you are linked to those who perpetrated it? Those who died in the Rwandan genocide knew their murderers personally. When a victim was killed, he or she was hacked or clubbed to death (as most were) by a neighbor, a colleague, a friend. Those who lived knew these killers just as intimately. They are the witnesses, connected to both the murdered and their murderers, a terrible connectedness that is almost impossible to move on from. This postscript is the story of just one such connection. It is the story of one man's death and all those linked to it, however desperately they wish they were not.

Before I wrote *The Overwhelming*, I did a year's worth of research. I read every book I could, learning the history and sequence of events surrounding the genocide. I memorized the layout of Kigali in 1994, studied the names of its streets, restaurants, bars; I taught myself simple words and rudimentary phrases in Kinyarwanda. But after I wrote a draft, I realized I couldn't go any further without having the play tested for authenticity. I needed to know if what I had written would ring true to Rwandans—to those who had actually lived through the events I was writing about.

Just as I found my writing stalled, my wife, Rebecca, was at a party in Cape Cod in March 2005 when she overheard someone talking about a doctor named Louis Kayitalire, a Rwandan genocide victim who now lived in Indiana. She asked for his e-mail address and passed it on to me; I then wrote and introduced myself. Would he be willing to read what I had written? Would he be honest with his criticism, even tear my play apart if he felt it required that?

Louis wrote back. He had escaped the killings in 1994 because he was in France on a medical residency. His father had written that things were getting dangerous at home and he was not to return. Louis stayed in Paris; his father and most of his mother's kin were murdered. "I would be honored," he wrote, "to help in any way to tell the story of what happened to my family and my country." I sent him the play and he quickly responded with scores of notes for me—a Tutsi surname attributed to a Hutu character, a misspelled street name, the subtle but key misuse of a saying in Kinyarwanda, and on and on. For months we wrote to each other and spoke on the phone as he critiqued my rewrites. We spoke for hours about the intricacies of Rwandan political and ethnic identity, about the hatred and fear that had engulfed his country. The talks were difficult for Louis. "I have worked very hard to put away these memories. To move forward with my life. It has been a struggle, but I am doing so."

Louis's dedication and expertise were a godsend, but how could I rely on the judgment and guidance of only one man? Just as I was stalled again, the PlayPenn new play workshop invited me to come to Philadelphia in July 2005 to work with a cast of actors and a director on *The Overwhelming*. They told me they'd learned of a Rwandan named Raymond Simba who taught Kinyarwanda part-time at the University of Pennsylvania. I wrote to Raymond asking if he too would read my play and, if it passed his muster, whether he would be willing to help me. He wrote back that he had been in Kigali when the genocide occurred and that he was eager to read what I had written. I sent it and he replied with reams of notes, translation and pronunciation corrections, and an offer to come to the workshop rehearsals and to teach the actors how to pronounce Kinyarwanda.

Raymond juggled his teaching and his job selling real estate to spend days with the cast and me. In a gentle voice barely above a whisper, he patiently taught the actors how to pronounce their lines. He graciously answered their questions about his country's history, the complexities of Hutu and Tutsi identity—and about the genocide itself. He told how his family had fled soon after the killings began, picking their way through the corpse-strewn streets. "It was a miracle," Raymond said. "Somehow, God knows, we were able to escape alive into Congo. From there I traveled to Senegal and then made my way here." Starting from nothing, he had taught himself English and begun his life anew in the United States. Repeatedly, Raymond thanked the actors for their hard work. "Doing this work, you will help prevent such horrors from ever taking place again. This is more important than you can know."

Quickly thereafter, in December 2005, the National Theatre in London agreed to mount the world premiere and to send me to Rwanda before rehearsals began. I called Louis to share the good news; he was overjoyed that I would get a chance to see his homeland. We made plans for me to visit him in his new house in Connecticut, where we would finally meet in person and celebrate our work together.

Then I called Raymond. Something in his voice was different, distant. "I am so sorry to have been out of touch, my friend. I have been traveling." He apologized for not returning my e-mail from a few weeks before with final, minute translation queries. I interrupted him. What was wrong? "I have been in Tanzania. At the genocide trials. My father has been accused."

Raymond had just returned from Arusha, Tanzania, where the International Criminal Tribunal for Rwanda was being held. He told me his father was imprisoned there, falsely accused of perpetrating genocide in 1994. "He was not even in that part of the country then. He was in the Gitarama, with me and the rest of our family, not in Gikongoro." The Rwandan government, he said, paid their witnesses to go testify against his father. But his father's witnesses were not even allowed to go to Tanzania to testify. "The government in Kigali is trying by all means to make him guilty."

Then, after all our months of conversation, Raymond spoke for the first time about his father. Aloys Simba was a retired soldier who had served in the army of the previous government. This was the same Hutu-dominated regime that planned and oversaw the genocide as part of its desperate fight against the RPF, a Tutsi-dominated guerrilla movement. But, his son said, Aloys Simba was simply a loyal soldier and a patriot. He had fought the RPF on the battlefield; that was all. But the RPF had won the war (which ended the genocide) and its leaders were now the backbone of the current Rwandan government. "The grudges," Raymond said, "even now they are still hard. My father has been framed. He has been found guilty of genocide. I do not know what I will do next."

Days later I drove up to Connecticut to meet Louis. He was as elegant and thoughtful in person as he was on the phone. We spent the afternoon looking at photos of his recent trip back to Rwanda and discussing whom he knew there that I should meet. As I got ready to leave, I asked him if I'd ever mentioned the other Rwandan who had been so helpful to me. I had not. I confided that this man had been in the back of my mind all day. "Sitting here talking with you," I said, "I keep thinking about what he and his family are going through right now, trying to come up with some way I can help." I began to tell Louis that the man's father was a military officer who had fought the RPF and had just been convicted of genocide in Arusha. Louis cut me off before I could continue.

"What was his name?" he asked sharply.

"Aloys Simba," I said.

His entire body recoiled.

"I know that name very well. That man killed my father."

Louis told me that his father's name was Joseph Kayihigi. He had been a doctor too. Joseph Kayihigi and Aloys Simba were good friends who had grown up together in Gikongoro, in the south of Rwanda. They were so close that Joseph was even Aloys's physician for a time. Later they both moved to Kigali, where their sons Louis and Raymond grew up as neighbors. Both fathers were Hutu, but Joseph had married a Tutsi. When the killings of Tutsis started, Joseph Kayihigi took his wife and their family back to Gikongoro. "My father hoped that those who knew him would not kill him as easily as strangers would," Louis said.

At the same time, Aloys Simba came out of retirement and was put in charge of the army in Gikongoro, to oversee the slaughter of Tutsis in his home prefecture and to fight the advancing forces of the RPF, Louis told me. When it became clear that the government army would lose, Simba forced all local Hutus to evacuate to Congo. When Aloys Simba came to Joseph Kayihigi's house,

Louis's father refused to evacuate on principle. "My father told Simba, 'This is my home, this is my country. *Your* hands are covered in blood. *You* must pay for it.' "

"The next night, Simba's men came around the house." Louis's voice rose and he cut the air with his hands as he continued. "This was on a direct order from Simba. No one in Gikongoro was touched without his say-so." Louis's father, uncle, and brother were dragged out into the street, denounced as traitors, and shot. "People were there. Many people, who all told me this." The other two men were killed instantly, but Louis's father was still alive. "My mother came out of hiding and realized that he was still living and bleeding from his chest. She sat next to her bleeding husband—next to the body of my brother, her dead son—desperate for help. None came. It took five hours for my father to die."

As the RPF advanced, Aloys Simba fled to Congo with his family, including Raymond, Louis said. They eventually made it to Senegal. Then Aloys Simba disappeared. "And how was Aloys Simba flown from Congo to Senegal?" Louis asked me, his eyes flashing. "Almost every high-ranking *Rwandais* who fled the killings and made it to Senegal was a *genocidaire*. Those protected by Hutu Power militias and then flown to safety by the French. I know this because I tried to pursue Simba on my own." For years Louis struggled to bring a case against Aloys Simba from his home in Paris. "But everywhere I turned, it was a dead end." Finally he had to stop and move on with his life. Here, from me, was the first he'd heard of Aloys Simba's arrest and conviction. He had been talking for an hour nonstop and his body was shaking. "You tell Raymond that one of the men who advises you is the son of Kayihigi. Man! You *see* what he says then."

All the next day I couldn't eat, couldn't work. I kept replaying the image of Louis's face as I said the name Aloys Simba and watched all color drain from it. I called him that evening and apologized for bringing such terrible memories back into his life.

"How could you know?" he asked. "The chance of this happening? Point zero, zero, zero one!" He spoke quickly, his voice pitched high, a torrent pouring out of him. "Since 1994, the time I have spent thinking about this man and how to get him! And then *you* would tell me this!" The memories had all flooded back. He could think of nothing else.

"I want to be very clear: I am not accusing Raymond of having anything to do with the genocide himself. The son is not guilty of the sins of the father." Still, he admitted, after I left, he had reread my play three times, rechecking all the Kinyarwanda in the script to make sure Raymond had not slipped in any secret Hutu Power words. "But, no. Your friend did an excellent job. He has served your work very well."

But what Louis could not forgive were what he called Raymond's lies. "That a man would stand by his father, this is expected. But that he would say that Aloys Simba is innocent. That his own escape to Congo—and beyond—was some 'miracle.' That he would pretend that this was not *proof* of his protection by the same thugs who did the murdering! He knows. He knows the truth about his dad."

Louis fell silent for a moment. When he spoke again, his voice was softer. "There is one thing. It is too much for me to see my name and the name Simba written together. If you choose to thank Raymond in your book instead of me, that is fine. He has clearly done good work. As for me, it was an honor to help you. That is enough. All I ask is this one favor. My family, people throughout Rwanda, if they see the names Louis Kayitalire and Raymond Simba thanked on the same page . . ." There was a long pause.

"J.T., they are not going to understand."

I got hold of a copy of the International Criminal Tribunal for Rwanda's indictment against retired Lieutenant Colonel Aloys Simba.* I also tracked down a copy of the court's summary of judgment that found him guilty. I discovered that Raymond's father had been one of eleven military officers who orchestrated the coup

**The Prosecutor v. Aloys Simba*, International Criminal Tribunal for Rwanda, Case No. ICTR-2001-76-I, Amended Indictment, May 10, 2004.

on July 5, 1973, that installed Juvénal Habyarimana as dictator of Rwanda—a corrupt reign that ended when Habyarimana's plane was mysteriously shot down on April 6, 1994, igniting the fuse of genocide. Raymond never told me that his father had been one of Habyarimana's closest confidants and one of the richest men in Rwanda. Raymond never told me that as he grew up in Kigali, his father's name was in every school textbook: he was one of the Comrades of the Fifth of July, a national hero.

The prosecution charged Aloys Simba with secretly helping to plan genocide and then coming out of retirement to lead the killings in Gikongoro and nearby Butare. He was accused of personally inciting genocide by rallying crowds to hunt and kill, and with overseeing the collecting and distributing of rifles and machetes with which to do so. Many witnesses backed up these charges. Over and over, they quoted Aloys Simba's own words. How he extolled his fellow Hutus to "get rid of the filth" that was their Tutsi neighbors. "The Tutsis have hatched a plot to kill the Hutus," he is said to have shouted as he urged his fellow citizens to butchery. "Therefore the Hutus must start the killings first."

Raymond's father was charged with overseeing the massacre at Kaduha Parish by grenade, gun, machete, and club. The killing went on for twelve hours. According to the indictment: "During the attack, which lasted the whole day, Aloys Simba replenished the ammunition of the attackers on several occasions." As I read on and on, I underlined the following sentences: "As a result of the attack, thousands of men, women and children were massacred . . . Many of the dead were buried between 23 April and 26 April 1994 in and around Kaduha."

I tracked down day-by-day accounts of Aloys Simba's trial from different African newspapers. They reported that the lieutenant colonel and his family fled Rwanda during the killings for Bukavu, Congo, and that Simba was finally arrested in Senegal in 2001. Simba means lion, they reported, and he was known as "the fearsome lion," feared by all. The articles made clear that the hero of the former regime had many defenders, even one who was "a renowned human rights activist in Rwanda before the 1994 genocide," but that his key witnesses' testimonies fell apart under cross-examination.

Aloys Simba was the last defense witness. He himself rejected all charges, arguing that he had in fact saved many Tutsis from death at the hands of others. His final, and by all accounts climactic, day of testimony was July 8, 2005. On that same day, his son was translating passages of my play and schooling me in the finer points of Rwandan culture and nuance. On that same day, Raymond spoke to me at length about the importance of the work I was doing. How he dearly hoped that telling this story would help prevent such awful violence from happening again.

Weeks later when I went to Kigali, I asked Rwandans from all walks of life about both fathers. Many people I spoke to knew of Joseph Kayihigi, that he had taught medicine at the university. I met men and women who had trained under him and spoke his name with reverence. Everyone I spoke to knew the name Aloys Simba. Without prompting, they spoke about his deeds during the genocide: the lion; the butcher; the man who came out of retirement just so he could get in some killing.

Aloys Simba was found guilty on December 13, 2005, on one count of genocide and one of crimes against humanity. He was sentenced to twenty-five years in prison. After all I've read and all those I've talked to, this seems to me to be a case of justice served. But the following facts from the summary of judgment must be acknowledged*:

1. The court ruled that the defense was hampered by not having enough time between the notice of the allegations and the trial.
2. Aloys Simba's sentence was reduced because he, unlike almost all other officials of the former government, acknowledged that a genocide had taken place and condemned it.

*_The Prosecutor v. Aloys Simba_, ICTR-2001-76-1, Summary of Judgment, December 13, 2005.

3. The court displayed further leniency because "his participation in the massacres [may have] resulted from misguided notions of patriotism and government allegiance rather than extremism or ethnic hatred."

It must also be acknowledged that every person I spoke with, from Louis onward, was far from an impartial witness. And there is also this: only days ago, Aloys Simba was granted the right to appeal his sentence. However much I may have read or heard, whatever opinions I may have formed, the question of Aloys Simba's guilt or innocence is still being wrestled with.

Finally, it must be acknowledged that while Louis has read and approved of how I have told this story, Raymond has not. I have called and written Raymond many times over the last six months but he has not responded. I do not know where, or how, he is.

There was a time when I fantasized about confronting Raymond, of demanding he come clean and tell me the truth. But such a fantasy is founded on a very American idea of confession and redemption. Like so much about Rwanda, there is no such redemption in this story. Raymond is still fighting to prove his father's innocence; Louis is still trying to move beyond his father's murder. Neither man can see beyond his own truth.

I have honored Louis's request: I thanked him in the earlier British edition of my play; Raymond is thanked in this one. I remain grateful to them both, but it is not for me to link their names together through my gratitude.

A country the size of Rwanda binds its people together in a way unimaginable to those of us living in the United States. When I tell other Americans that here, in a country of 300 million people, a Rwandan I met by chance in Indiana and a Rwandan I met by chance in Pennsylvania turned out to have grown up on the same street in Kigali and that their lives and histories are inextricably linked by blood, they can hardly believe it. But when I told this story in Kigali, no one batted an eye.

The murder of Joseph Kayihigi was a grievous and terrible loss.

I have found myself caught up in the story of his death, but also in the stories of those still living who are struggling to move on. Because as I write this story, the repercussions of Joseph Kayihigi's death still ripple outward, marking the lives of his family, friends, enemies, and strangers, on at least three continents. I think of his killing and all it has wrought daily. And when I do, I remind myself that his death was one of eight hundred thousand.

J. T. ROGERS
Brooklyn, N.Y.
May 20, 2007

Rwanda—"Never Again"

BY FERGAL KEANE

Fergal Keane covered the Rwandan genocide for BBC News and wrote a memoir of this experience, Season of Blood

I have some good friends in the village of Nyarubuye, in southeast Rwanda on the border with Tanzania. It is a remote place, several miles up a dirt track in the stony hills overlooking the Akagera River and the East African savannah. The person who is closest to me is a twenty-year-old girl named Valentina who survived the Rwandan genocide by hiding amid the bodies of her murdered family and friends. They were murdered by her Hutu neighbors and local police and soldiers acting on the orders of the mayor.

In the year before the catastrophe, she was a teenage girl hoping to move from her village school to a good secondary education. I use the conditional advisedly. As a Tutsi, Valentina was not guaranteed a proper education. She belonged to a minority who had been discriminated against and brutalized since Rwanda gained independence from Belgium in the early 1960s.

Tutsis were shut out of any meaningful role in the government, denied places at university, excluded from the civil service. There were exceptions, but the general picture was grim. After the Tutsi-dominated rebel movement, the Rwandan Patriotic Front, invaded in 1990, attempting to force the government into a more democratic dispensation, the level of oppression against Tutsis increased dramatically.

As Hutu extremism became the dominant political ideology, so, too, did the idea of a great extermination gain credence as the answer to the "Tutsi problem." Genocide became state policy. While the president talked peace with the rebels, his acolytes trained a militia to destroy the minority. All the organs of state were harnessed to this end, most notably the security forces and the media. Radio and newspapers demonized the Tutsis. For some, the ruling elite's Tutsi-hating did not go far enough. Extremist opposition parties grew up with their own radio station and newspapers and their own militia.

In the daily life of Nyarubuye, a community of peasant farmers and cattle herders, a place far from the city, it would have been difficult to detect just how dramatically the situation was changing in the early months of 1994. The local Tutsis had heard the radio broadcasts and noticed the militia being trained. The older ones would have experienced pogroms in 1959, again in the 1960s, and also in 1973. But none expected a calamity on the scale of what was being planned by the extremists who now controlled Rwanda.

Valentina does remember that in the months before the genocide, the atmosphere in her village began to change. Her parents tried to protect her from the poison being spread on the radio. But Hutu children at school began to make nasty remarks. The word "foreigner" was being used to denigrate the Tutsis. There were mocking comments about people with long noses and fingers. (Hutu extremists claimed that the Tutsis were invaders who had come from the Horn of Africa centuries before.) Worst of all, the Hutu teachers were indoctrinating their pupils with anti-Tutsi poison, singling out children like Valentina every time they taught Rwandan history.

The French historian of the genocide, Gérard Prunier, has a wonderful phrase to describe Rwanda in the months leading up to the explosion of violence. Rwanda, he writes, was "a claustrophobic, airless hell." A small elite, determined to preserve its power, was manipulating resentment into hatred, feeding on the fear of the Tutsi rebels, telling the Hutus they would be enslaved once more, as in the old days, when Belgian colonialists used Tutsi aristocrats to enforce their rule. In this tiny country, where Hutus and Tutsis lived crowded together on the green hills, the hatred was spreading like fire. The UN force that had been deployed to monitor a supposed peace and transition to a kind of democratic politics could see what was happening. But the warnings sent to New York, the appeal for a tougher approach to the extremists, went ignored by the high officials of the organization. As the spring approached and incidents of violence increased, the architects of Rwanda's apocalypse simply waited for their moment.

When it came, on April 6, with the shooting-down of President Habyarimana's plane as it approached the Kigali airport, the speed of the killing stunned the small UN force. By the time the genocide ended on July 4, some eight hundred thousand people had been murdered by machete, ax, gun, and grenade. In Nyarubuye, Valentina fled with her family to the local church. Within days it was surrounded and attacked by her Hutu neighbors. She watched as boys she had grown up with in the village hacked her loved ones to death.

Journalists have told some of the story of Rwanda. So, too, have historians. But I know that theater can reach an audience, and convey truths, with a power that can elude those of us who operate in the strict language of the news bulletin or the newspaper dispatch. This play deals with Rwanda as it was in the early months of 1994, perched on the edge of the volcano. It was a time when the world knew very little of Rwanda or of the lives of children like Valentina. A play can entertain, challenge, upset, and anger an audience; at its best, it can make them think deeply about the world in which they live and be prepared to challenge orthodoxies and lies. This play is a powerful antidote to the kind of indifference that characterized our response to Rwanda. It is a call to action for those who care about the horrors currently being perpetrated against innocent people in Darfur, a reminder that if you believe in the words "never again," you cannot simply leave the theater feeling moved and inspired and allow those feelings to dissipate. Involve yourself in the fight for human rights. There are plenty of good organizations, like Human Rights Watch and Amnesty International, whose existence is our best hope of preventing another Rwanda. It really is *our* responsibility.

FERGAL KEANE
May 2006

"Just Words"

In February 2006, the director Max Stafford-Clark and I flew to Rwanda. Neither of us had been before, and we were keen to visit before the start of rehearsals for the play's premiere at the National Theatre in London. I had written *The Overwhelming* based on research and interviews with expatriate Rwandais living in the United States. Having a chance to talk face to face with residents of Kigali and to walk the streets and visit the houses and buildings where my play takes place would show me what I had gotten right—and wrong.

We spent a week living in Kigali, traveling all over the city and to villages throughout the center of the country. We met and spoke with an extraordinary number of Rwandais from all walks of life. Some would talk on the record, some only off. All were remarkably forthcoming and generous with their time and insights. Our goal was to focus our questions on the Rwanda, and specifically Kigali, of early 1994, when the play takes place—and before most people had an inkling of the scope of the horrors to come. But that was not what people wanted to speak about. Once they answered our questions, they wanted to talk about the genocide itself: why it happened, what they experienced, and how they were living with what they had seen and done. They spoke sometimes for hours on end. They needed to speak; we were asked to bear witness.

Later, while we rehearsed the play in London, we interviewed other survivors of the genocide as well as journalists who covered it. They, too, quickly steered our discussions to their own personal experiences. They, too, needed to speak, wanting what they had seen and learned to be known.

Here are excerpts from some of the people Max and I interviewed. These are their words, transcribed by me.

WE WERE LIVING ALWAYS IN FEAR

We Tutsi were given names of insects, animals, viruses, snakes. If you are constantly told this, subconsciously you start to believe. You start to feel less than a human being. There was an intellectual genocide before the physical one. Tutsi were shut out of all important jobs. In a Tutsi family, only the weakest one was allowed to continue on in school. Tutsi were scapegoats when politicians needed scapegoats. A common enemy is easy: all will be on your side. This is much easier than a political solution. As the RPF formed, then attacked, Hutu here said: "If we had killed all the Tutsi before, we wouldn't have these problems now!" Yes, the Hutu chanted, "Tuzabat sembat semba!"—"We will exterminate them!"—in the streets, but we thought it was just words.

—JEAN GAKWANDI, *director of Solace Ministries*

I was a doctor for five years at Kigali Hospital. In October 1990, the weekend of the RPF's first attack, during the bombing, we had to operate all night on patients without anesthetics. It was very hard. At the end of it, my colleague turned to me and said, "What is Habyarimana waiting for? If he says kill Tutsis, I will—starting with you!"

—SENATOR ODETTE NYIRAMILIMO

The Interahamwe used to run practice drills in front of the CND [Parliament building] to intimidate us. They would hurl insults.

There was talk of killing people, but nothing like genocide. We had studied history, but we were taken by surprise by the extent of the killings.

—GENERAL CHARLES KAYONGA,
commander of the RPF troops stationed in the CND before and during the genocide

I thought when it finally came, they would kill the politicians. But not one million people. Not women and babies!

—JEAN-PIERRE SAGAHUTU

LOOK, THE TRUTH IS MESSY

You can hardly differentiate between Tutsi and Hutu. I myself can barely tell. That's why they had identity cards! Just as I can't differentiate Europeans—French? English? Italian? That's why, during the genocide, very many Hutu died. Someone is tall, they are comparing noses. They see you, and you are killed. And yet maybe you are a Hutu.

—VÉNUSTE KARASIRA

We speak the same languages, we live in the same villages. Tutsis are tall and thin? Look at me, I am not tall or thin! Even ourselves, we are lost determining who is what.

—DR. VINCENT BIRUTA,
president of Rwanda's senate

Look, the truth is messy. The truth is that most Hutus were perpetrators *and* bystanders *and* protectors—it all depended on the day and the situation. Every Hutu was involved in every part of the genocide. Every one. They had no choice, not if they wanted to live.

—ANONYMOUS

IT WAS SYSTEMATIC

It was systematic. Taxi drivers killed taxi drivers, doctors killed doctors. All knew each other here. Colleagues killed colleagues. My father was a doctor. Another doctor killed him.

—JEAN-PIERRE SAGAHUTU

Those who organized the genocide used the tool of using everybody. If everyone is guilty, there is impunity. At the end of the day, who are you going to punish?

—GEOFFREY NGIRUWONSANGA,
Program Manager, Survivors Fund

People were told, kill as many as possible. Whatever you kill, you occupy. This is why there was massive participation with the poor people. It was like a competition.

—VÉNUSTE KARASIRA

THEY CUT LIKE THEY WERE CUTTING FLOWERS

My husband was killed on the night of April 7, 1994. My mother and two children were killed. My children were burned alive. I was alone with my nine-month-old. Killers found me hiding. "Come, we will help you," they said. Then they raped me. No one would help me. I was an animal in front of them . . . I was alone on the road for three days. I could not walk. A man came by and said, "You will die, not with a gun but painfully." He took me home and passed the time raping me. In the morning he took my baby, he took him to a big tree and beat his head, here and here, then hung him by the feet. Then he let him down, but he was already dead. I was made to dig the grave. After three weeks walking at night to find relatives. No food. No water. When I got there, they were all dead. I lay down and slept for three days. Kids fetching water found me and said, "Oh, here is an old woman," but I was twenty-three. I had spent three weeks looking for death, but I had not found it. By my looks, everyone feared to come near me . . . I was white. They thought I was a spirit.

—SARAFINA

The day the president's plane was shot down, young people came to my house. "You people killed our president, and we will kill you." But we thought it was a joke, a mockery. These were our neighbors. My husband said, "We are safe; they will not kill." A group of Interahamwe came, and they cut like they were cutting flowers. My husband and five of my children were lain on the ground, in a line, and they were killed.

—AGNES

During the genocide, my family was killed, and I was raped and kept as a sex slave for four weeks by a gang of Interahamwe. I was lucky that I was taken by one who was strong and not shared by five or twenty. I was locked in a house all day while they were out killing; then they came home, and I would be raped. I never knew if I would be killed, too. We had a family of not less than a thousand people. The whole village was made up of my family. Today there are only fifteen.

—MARGARITA

I've been places with malevolent forces—people—before, but here it felt like the moral energy of the place had been sucked out and nothing had replaced it. It really felt like right was wrong and wrong was right. You could *hear* the leaves whispering—very bad things. All your senses were attenuated. The first day was very difficult. Dead people wherever you went: ditches, banana groves, schools. You walked into a school and saw piles of bodies. Houses of murdered Tutsi were entirely stripped, down to the wiring. Almost like soldier ants going through a body. It was medieval, really.

Inexplicable. At a church we saw, I kept imagining God sitting on the roof, looking down on the bedlam. And then I imagined the devil was there with Him, dancing gleefully. "Look at what I'm doing!"

—DAVID BELTON,
former journalist and producer of the film Beyond the Gates, *interviewed in London*

I was in hiding for two months and sixteen days, in an empty septic tank in Nyamirambo. I lost forty kilos. I came out only at two A.M., to try and find food and to stretch. I spent the days and nights hunched over, unable to move or stand. It was always loud, from the killings. Finally, one day it was so quiet I came out during the day. I saw soldiers and knew I was going to die. So I shouted at them, taunting them so that they would become so angry they would shoot me quickly and not cut me slowly with machetes. But they were not the government soldiers, they were RPF. I did not know the war was over.

—JEAN-PIERRE SAGAHUTU

I dreaded going back, but I *had* to go back. This was June, after a month away. The country was empty. We flew to Goma and got there just ahead of a column of two million people who came through a corridor the size of this room, nonstop for two days. They were terrifying and dangerous: a beaten army who *knew* what they had done. I know they knew because I asked them.

—DAVID BELTON

I HAVE NOT TOLD ANYONE THIS

Forty percent of the women survivors were raped during the genocide. It was organized, a tool. Deliberate, this infection of HIV. Only peasant women will admit to being raped. Wealthier women, they won't talk about it. In our culture, we don't talk about sex, even forced sex. It's a taboo. They are ashamed to ask for help. If they do seek counseling, they end up seeing their tormentors. They go, they stand in a line—the same line with the men who raped them, or those men's wives. The survivor says, "I would rather go hungry and die than stand with these people."

—GABO WILSON,
Rwanda country director, Survivors Fund

There is a phenomenon here of survivors' guilt among the Tutsi who lived through the killings. Especially among women who were not raped or disfigured. This feeling that they got off easy, that they wish, in a twisted way, that they *had* been raped. One of the saddest things I've ever seen.

—HELEN VESPIRINI, *Agence France-Presse*

I had a child by my rapist. Working here, being helped by social workers, this is what taught me finally to love my child for the first time. This is why I have trained and become a social worker myself. But I have just tested positive for HIV. I am trying to be strong, but deep in my heart of hearts, I am asking—Why? Why? Why? I am told my child tested negative, but I think the doctors only told me that because they felt sorry. I have not told anyone else this. I cannot tell my family because I am supporting all of them. If they knew, they would lose all hope and sunlight. I have always liked acting and always wanted to be an actor. This is why I am telling you this. The theater is important for this—to tell this.

—MARGARITA

THE VICTIMS WILL NEVER FORGET

I live here with my sisters, Beatrice and Joseanne. I am the head of the family. Our parents were killed in 1994. During the genocide. They were thrown in a lake. We saw this. I exchanged my life for my sisters', so they could have a better life. I take care of the gardens and try to make sure there is food to eat when my sisters come back from school. I till the land, I sell soap and salt. It was very hard at first to become used to all the responsibility. At first we had no money. I was selling tomatoes, and people were buying them not because they wanted tomatoes but because they were supporting me. My sisters may not appreciate what I do, but they do not have a problem with it, either. When they finish school, I think they will help me to learn a trade and be a tailor.

—DROCELLA NYIRANEZA, *age twenty-two*

What we are seeking is a repatriation of memory. We are testimony that the genocide happened. There is no way we live the way we do without a genocide. The victims will never forget. The more you think and talk about it, there is a slow healing. If not, it will just erupt.

—ODETTE KAYIRERE,
Coordinatrice Région Est,
Association des Veuves du Génocide Agahozo

A FIRE UNDERGROUND

I'm sorry I keep looking over my shoulder before answering your questions. It's a habit we have here.

—ANONYMOUS

I was there. This eight hundred thousand—this is not true. Four hundred thousand, at most. This is how many that died. The RPF took my country only to take the Congo. Where is the talk of that? It is all about money and power; they had to get to the Congo, as Rwanda has nothing. This is what you must understand: It was a war, not a genocide. All these dead bodies lying around after the war was over—tell me, who would leave their families like that? Not bury them like that? This was a plot. These bodies were placed there. Propaganda. It is very simple: The RPF wanted wealth. They passed as Hutu to do this killing. The Tutsi are clever. Please do not say that I said this.

—A HUTU SURVIVOR, *interviewed in London*

These killers convicted and imprisoned in Arusha, with their so-called human rights. They have Internet! They have everything! It is just that they are not with their families. Otherwise, they are okay.

—A GENOCIDE SURVIVOR

So my question is, how do you get past it, when every street is framed with communal bloodletting? This wasn't Jews being secreted off to be gassed in Poland—it was all in plain sight.

—DAVID BELTON

Could it happen here again? I don't think so. It was the Hutu Power leadership that supported all that. This government of reconciliation gives us hope. Once the older generation passes, once we are all gone, I believe Hutu and Tutsi will be a problem of the past.

—A SURVIVOR

Now it is two hundred percent safe here. But until when, I don't know. Rwanda is like a fire underground: The killings will come again.

—ANOTHER SURVIVOR

It happened, therefore it can happen again:
this is the core of what we have to say.
It can happen, and it can happen anywhere.

—PRIMO LEVI,
The Drowned and the Saved